CW00552852

SERVE TO LEAD

SERVE TO LEAD

The British Army's Manual of Leadership

Indie*Books*

Acknowledgements

The publishers are grateful to the following organizations for their permission and advice regarding the reprinting of extracts in this book:

The Random House Group Ltd for excerpts reprinted from The Edge of the Sword by Capt. Anthony Farrar-Hockley, published by Frederick Muller; and from The Monastery by Fred Majdalany, published by Bodley Head.

HarperCollins and David Higham Associates for their advice relating to the reprinting of extracts from The Wild Green Earth by Brig. Bernard Fergusson and Years of Victory by Sir Arthur Bryant.

Continuum for their advice regarding The Commander by Gen. Sir Ian Hamilton, published by Hollis & Carter.

Orion Publishing Group for their advice relating to the reprinting of extracts from Courage and other Broadcasts and Defeat into Victory by Field Marshal Viscount Slim, published by Cassell.

In the remaining cases, where copyright is applicable, all attempts at tracing the copyright holders were unsuccessful.

Serve to Lead:
The British Army's Manual of Leadership

Introduction by Robin Matthews

ISBN: 978-1-908041-02-9

Published by IndieBooks Ltd
4 Staple Inn, London, WC1V 7QH
www.indiebooks.co.uk

This edition © IndieBooks 2014

Printed by TJ International Ltd, Padstow, Cornwall, PL28 8RW

CONTENTS

Robin Matthews is a former British Army Officer. An unlikely graduate of the Royal Military Academy Sandhurst, he went on to command his Regiment, The Light Dragoons, which included a tour of duty in Iraq in 2005. Prior to leaving the Army at the beginning of 2009, he also served with 16 (Air Assault) Brigade in Helmand Province, Afghanistan. He is now an entrepreneur and is currently working with an American energy, water and food security company. He is married with three children and lives in Bath.

INTRODUCTION

SERVE TO LEAD is a remarkable book. Produced by the Royal Military Academy Sandhurst after the Second World War, it is as clear and concise a treatise on leadership as you will find; it also provides a fascinating glimpse into what sets the Profession of Arms apart from any other. When you read this, the original version, you will see that it is curiously edited, a little uneven and old fashioned – quaint even. Minor quibbles aside, it is full of charm. And, for those who have served, it is a memento to their youth and the overcoming of testing times, which in pushing people to their limits showed more clearly than anything just how far they might go. Only recently updated, it has inspired countless generations of British Army Officer.

Serve to Lead is synonymous with Sandhurst, placed on the bed of every officer cadet at the beginning of their military training. Somewhere between prayer book (which is what I thought it was initially) and bible (as it has often been referred), it lays out what is expected, and what to expect.

Unequivocally, it establishes selflessness, self-discipline, integrity and duty as the bedrock of leadership; excitingly, it speaks of courage and boldness as the essential differentiators, upon which events turn, and to which soldiers and leaders are instinctively drawn.

"….to dare boldly,
In a fair cause, and for their country's safety:
to run upon the cannon's mouth undaunted;.." (p54)

Slim and unobtrusive, but distinctive nevertheless, it is the perfect handrail for the young, confident, but as yet not wholly formed men and women embarking on Sandhurst's grueling programme of leadership training, as so many of us did, during a profound period of personal change. Looking back, I am taken with the idea that somehow **Serve to Lead** was there by our beds, available for quiet contemplation and reflection when required. In truth, the intensity of training is such that moments like that were rare and when they did come were all too often overtaken by deep sleep. Leadership is the dominant theme at Sandhurst, but sleep comes a very close second. Fortunately, like the piles of uniform pushed across the quartermaster's counter on your first day, **Serve to Lead** is also for the keeping. So when the long trail of cars carrying newly commissioned officers speeds out the Sandhurst gates for the last time, a copy is more than likely to have been stowed neatly into the corner of a heavy rucksack. Largely untouched for the previous nine months, everyone knows that it may yet come in handy.

And so it does, for **Serve to Lead** comes into its own after Sandhurst. Regardless of rank or position there is always something to dip into. For the young officer, leading soldiers for the first time, the section on the British Soldier guides and inspires in equal measure. For those in more senior positions, Slim's beautifully simple thoughts on the foundations of morale are like a magnet; so too Nelson's thoughts on enlightened discipline. And for those with loftier ambition, looking to measure themselves against the great wartime commanders, who dominated the intellectual landscape of the post-war years, the eternal question: would I a Slim or Monty be? Or a Wellington, whose small but watchful portrait hung behind my desk while commanding my regiment a decade and a half or so after leaving Sandhurst; and whose famous dictum, was as sure a guard against complacency and self-congratulation as anything. "My rule was always to do the business of the day in the day." Today, my hope is that there was the odd day when I didn't disappoint the 'Old Nosey'. But equally, and rightly, those charged with shaping the present can never escape the ghosts of the past. In this respect, Serve to Lead precisely hits the mark.

Of course, not everyone who graduates from Sandhurst pursues a long military career; many leave after a few years to follow other paths. However, regardless of what happens afterwards, the common consent at subsequent reunions is always that Sandhurst set the standard. And that standard is as neatly encapsulated in this slim and elegant book, as it is anywhere. *Serve to Lead* is of course painted on a military canvas, but its instruction around leadership is timeless and has universal application.

The CEO of a start-up business; the Head of an underperforming school; the board of a charity or hospital trust: all are or should be just as concerned with courage, people and morale as any military commander. It is therefore to be welcomed, that the kernel of the British Army's leadership training, so admired globally, gets the long overdue chance to speak to a wider audience. There is much to enjoy and consider on every page, but the most beguiling message of the book concerns humility. Leadership must be confident, but unless it is matched in equal measure by humility, it jars, at which point the led simply fall away. If I am to lead you, first and foremost I must be your servant. Like any good book, the clue is in the title: in this case, simple, seemingly contradictory, but ultimately profound – Serve to Lead.

Robin Matthews
June 2013

PREFACE

"It is the fact that some men possess an inbred superiority which gives them a dominating influence over their contemporaries' and marks them out unmistakably for leadership. This phenomenon is as certain as it is mysterious. It is apparent in every association of human beings in every variety of circumstances and on every plane of culture. In a school among the boys, in a college among the students' in a factory, shipyard, or mine among the workmen, as certainly as in the Church and in the Nation, there are those who, with an assured and unquestioned title, take the leading place, and shape the general conduct."

The Lord Bishop of Durharm, Walker Trust Lecture on Leadership 1934, before the University of St Andrews.

"The safety and honour of Britain depend not on her wealth and administration, but on the character of her people. This in turn on the institutions which form character of her people. In war, it depends in particular, on the military institutions which create the martial habits of discipline, courage, loyalty, pride and endurance."

Sir Arthur Bryant in an article, "The Fate of the Regime" Times, 4th April, 1948.

MORALE

The Essentials of Morale

Morale is a state of mind. It is that intangible force which will move a whole group of men to give their last ounce to achieve something, without counting the cost to themselves; that makes them feel they are part of something greater than themselves. If they are to feel that, their morale must, if it is to endure — and the essence of morale is that it should endure — have certain foundations. These foundations are spiritual, intellectual, and material, and that is the order of their importance. Spiritual first, because only spiritual foundations can stand real strain. Next intellectual, because men are swayed by reason as well as feelings. Material last — important, but last — because the very highest kind of morale are often met when material conditions are lowest.

I remember sitting in my office and tabulating these foundations of morale something like this:

1. Spiritual
(a) There must be a great and noble object.
(b) Its achievement must be vital.
(c) The method of achievement must be active, aggressive.
(d) A man must feel that what he is and what he does matters directly towards the attainment of the object.

2. Intellectual
(a) He must be convinced that the object can be attained; that it is not out of reach.
(b) He must see, too, that the organisation to which he belongs and which is striving to attain the object is an efficient one.
(c) He must have confidence in his leaders and know that what-

ever dangers and hardships he is called to suffers, his life will
not be lightly flung away.

3. Material
(a) The man must feel that he will get a fair deal from his commanders and from the army generally.
(b) He must, as far as humanly possible, be given the best weapons and equipment for his task.
(c) His living and working conditions must be made as good
as they can be.

It was one thing thus neatly to marshal my principles but quite
another to develop them, apply them, and get them recognised by
the whole army.

At any rate our spiritual foundation was a firm one. I use the
word spiritual, not in its strictly religious meaning, but as a belief
in a cause. Religion has always been and still is one of the greatest
foundations of morale, especially of military morale. Saints and
soldiers have much in common. The religion of the Mohammed-
an, of the Sikh, of the Gurkha, and of the fighting Hindu . . . can
rouse in men a blaze of contempt for death. The Christian religion
is above all others a source of that enduring courage which is the
most valuable of all the components of morale.

Yet religion, as we understand it, is not essential to high morale. Anyone who has fought with or against Nazi paratroopers,
Japanese suicide squads, or Russian Commissars, will have found
this; but a spiritual foundation, belief in a cause, there must be.

We had this. . . . If ever an army fought in a just cause we did.
We coveted no man's country; we wished to impose no form of
government on any nation. We fought for the clean, the decent,
the free things of life, for the right to live our lives in our own way,
as others could live theirs, to worship God in what faith we chose,
to be free in body and mind, and for our children to be free. We
fought only because the powers of evil had attacked these things. . .

The fighting soldier facing the enemy can see that what he does, whether he is brave or craven, matters to his comrades and directly influences the result of the battle. It is harder for the man working on the road far behind, the clerk checking stores in a dump, the head-quarters' telephone operator monotonously plugging through his calls . . . the Quartermaster's orderly issuing bootlaces in a reinforcement camp — it is hard for these and a thousand others to see that they too matter. Yet everyone . . . in the army . . . had to be made to see where his task fitted into the whole, to realise what depended on it, and to feel pride and satisfaction in doing it well.

Now these things, while the very basis of morale, because they were purely matters of feeling and emotion, were the most difficult to put over, especially to the British portion of the army. . . . I felt there was only one way to do it, by a direct approach to the men themselves. Not by written exhortations, by wireless speeches, but by informal talks and contacts between troops and commanders. There was nothing new in this; my Corps and Divisional commanders and others right down the scale were already doing it. . .

. . . We, my commanders and I, talked to units, to collections of officers, to headquarters, to little groups of men, to individual soldiers casually met as we moved around. And we all talked the same stuff with the same object. Whenever I could get away from my head-quarters, and throughout the campaign was about a third of the time, I was in these first few months more like a parliamentary candidate than a general except I never made a promise.

I learnt, too, that one did not need to be an orator to be effective. Two things only were necessary: first to know what you were talking about, and, second and most important, to believe it yourself. I found that if one kept the bulk of one's talk to the material things the men were interested in, food, pay, leave, beer, mails, and the progress of operations, it was safe to end on a higher note — the spiritual foundations — and I always did.

To convince the men in the less spectacular or less obviously important jobs that they were very much part of the army, my commanders — and I made it our business to visit these units, to show an interest in them, and to tell them how we and the rest of the army depended upon them. There are in the army, and for that matter any big organisation, very large numbers of people whose existence is only remembered when something for which they are responsible goes wrong. Who thinks of the telephone operator until he fails to get his connection, of the cipher officer until he makes a mistake in his decoding, of the orderlies carry papers about a big headquarters until they take them to the wrong people, of the cook until he makes a particularly foul mess of the interminable bully? Yet they are important. . . .

We played on this very human desire of every man to feel himself and his work important, until one of the most striking things about our army was the way the administrative, labour, and non-combatant units acquired a morale which rivalled that of the fighting formations. They felt they shared directly in the triumphs of the Fourteenth Army and that its success and its honour were in their hands as much as anybody's. Another way in which we made every man feel he was part of the show was by keeping him, whatever his rank, as far as was practicable in the picture of what was going on around him. . . .

It was in these ways we laid the spiritual foundations, but that was not enough; they would have crumbled without others, the intellectual and the material. Here we had first to convince the doubters that our object, the destruction of the Japanese Army in battle, was practicable. . . . It had to be demonstrated practically. . . A victory in a large-scale battle was, in our present state of training, organisation, and confidence, not to be attempted. We had first to get the feel through the army that it was we who were hunting the Jap, not he us.

All commanders therefore directed their attention to patrolling. In jungle warfare this is the basis of success. It not only gives eyes to the side that excels at it, and blinds its opponent, but through it the soldier learns to move confidently in the elements in which he works. Every forward unit, not only infantry, chose its best men, formed patrols, trained and practised them, and then sent them out on business. . .These patrols came back to their regiments with stories of success. . . .The stories lost nothing in the telling, and there was no lack of competition for the next patrol. . . .

In about 90 per cent of these tiny patrol actions we were successful. By the end of November our forward troops had gone a long way towards getting that individual feeling of superiority and that first essential in the fighting man — the desire to close with his enemy. . . .

Having developed the confidence of the individual man in his superiority over the enemy, we had now to extend that to the corporate confidence of units and formations in themselves. This was done in a series of carefully planned minor offensive operations, carried out as the weather improved, against enemy advanced detachments. These were carefully staged, ably led, and, as I was always careful to ensure, in greatly preponderating strength. . . . Besides, we could not at this stage risk even small failures. We had very few, and the individual superiority built up by more successful patrolling grew into a feeling of superiority within units and formations. We were then ready to undertake larger operations. We had laid the first of our intellectual foundations of morale; everyone knew we could defeat the Japanese; our object was attainable.

The next foundation, that the men should feel that they belonged to an efficient organisation, that Fourteenth Army was well run and would get somewhere, followed partly from these minor successes. . . . Rations did improve, though still far below what they should be; mail began to arrive more regularly; there were even signs of a welfare service. An innovation was to be the publication of a theatre newspaper — SEAC. . . .

One of the greatest weakeners of morale had been the state of the rest and reinforcement camps. In these camps on the line of communications all reinforcements to the various fronts were held often for weeks until required. Almost without exception I found these places depressing beyond words. Decaying tents, or dilapidated bashas, with earth floors, mosquito ridden and lacking all amenities, were the usual accommodation; training and recreation were alike unorganised; men were crowded together from all units. No wonder spirits sank, discipline sagged, and defeatist rumours spread. Worst of all, the commandants and staffs, with a few notable exceptions, were officers and NCOs who were not wanted by units or who preferred the rear to the front. This lamentable state of affairs had to be taken in hand at once. The first step was to choose an officer with energy, experience, and organising ability to take overall charge. . . . The next step was to select really good officers to command and staff the camps. . . . Each camp was allotted to a forward division. That division provided its officers and instructors; the divisional flag was flown and its sign worn. Divisional commanders were encouraged to visit their camps, and from the moment a man arrived he was made to feel that he belonged to a fighting formation in which he could take pride. Training became real, discipline was reasserted, and in a few months the Fourteenth Army reinforcement camps . . . were clean, cheerful, active parts of the Army.

A most potent factor in spreading this belief in the efficiency of an organisation is a sense of discipline. In effect, discipline means that every man) when things pass beyond his own authority or initiative, knows to whom to turn for further direction. If it is the right kind of discipline he turns in the confidence that he will get sensible and effective direction. Every step must be taken to build up this confidence of the soldier in his leaders. For instance, it is not enough to be efficient; the organisation must look efficient. If you enter the lines of a regiment where the Quarter Guard is smart and alert, and the men you meet are well turned out and salute briskly, You cannot fail to get an impression of efficiency. You are right; ten to one that unit is efficient. If you go into a Headquarters and find the clerks scruffy, the floor unswept, and dirty tea-mugs staining fly-blown papers on office tables, it may be efficient but no visitors will think so.

We tried to make our discipline intelligent, but we were an old-fashioned army and we insisted on outward signs. . . . We expected soldiers to salute officers and officers to salute in return — both in mutual confidence and respect. I encouraged all officers to insist whenever possible, and there were few places where it was not possible, on good turn out and personal cleanliness. It takes courage, especially for a young officer, to check a man met on the road for not saluting properly or for slovenly appearance, but, every time he does, it adds to his stock of moral courage, and whatever the soldier may say he has a respect for the officer who does pull him up. . . .

(Thus) the intellectual foundations of morale were laid. There remained the material. . . . Material conditions, though lamentably low by the standards of any other British army, were improving.

Yet I knew that whatever had been promised . . . from home, it would be six months at least before it reached my troops. We would remain, for a long time yet, desperately short. . . .

These things were frankly put to the men by their commanders at all levels and, whatever their race, they responded. In my experience it is not so much asking men to fight or work with inadequate or obsolete equipment that lowers morale but the belief that those responsible are accepting such a state of affairs. If men realise that everyone above them and behind them is flat out to get the things required for them, they will do wonders, as my men did, with the meagre resources they have instead of sitting down moaning for better.

I do not say that the men of the Fourteenth Army welcomed difficulties, but they grew to take a fierce pride in overcoming them by determination and ingenuity. From start to finish they had only two items of equipment that were never in short supply;

their brains and their courage. They lived up to the unofficial motto I gave them, "God helps those who help themselves". Anybody could do an easy job we told them. It would take real men to overcome the shortages and difficulties we should be up against the tough chap for the tough job. . .

In these and many other ways we translated my rough notes on the foundations of morale, spiritual, intellectual, and material, into a fighting spirit for our men and a confidence in themselves and their leaders that was to impress our friends and surprise our enemies.

Field-Marshal Sir William Slim, Defeat into Victory

Morale in Battle

High morale is a quality without which no war can be won. It is therefore a vital quality.

We must first understand what we mean by "morale". This is wrapped up in the human factor, since the raw material with which we soldiers have to deal is "men".

The Human Factor

I would like to begin by giving you my general views about the nature of our Army. One great lesson stands out clearly in my mind from the late war, in which we went through some very bad times but stood up undaunted, and then hit back. It is this. The true and ultimate strength of a nation lies in its people, in their capacity to work, in their virility. It lies, in fact, in the national character. It is this national character that produces the fighting man — the soldier.

The soldier is not chiefly a military figure; he is primarily a social figure. He is influenced by his home, his upbringing, and his historical traditions. He is a soldier only because military training has imposed a certain fixed pattern of behaviour upon him. The soldier is, in fact, a citizen of the nation. The Army is woven into the social fabric of the nation and is an integral part of the community. No matter what may be instilled into him in the Army, the soldier will retain his individual character, which he derives from his environment. He will reflect, primarily, the national character of his country. The national character is therefore of immense importance. Anything that weakens the national character weakens the Army. An army is not, and never can be merely a collection of individuals. It is a fighting weapon moulded by discipline and controlled by leaders. The aim of an army is to achieve success in battle against the enemies of the nation. All training must be directed towards his end, and it must never be forgotten even though the country is at peace. Training must from the earliest days concentrate on the selection of leaders and the infusion of discipline. It is by discipline that an army is welded into a fighting weapon; it is by leadership that it is led to victory. These are the fundamental factors which affect the morale of the soldier and lead to success in battle.

The Quality of Morale

In war the moral stature of some men increases, and their characters grow stronger and more closely knit in proportion to the discomforts and dangers they are called upon to face. Such men will occasionally perform in battle remarkable acts of selfless courage and daring, and will endure with extraordinary fortitude and patience the burdens thrust upon them. Other men, however, will under the stress of hardships or dangers surrender to fear or fatigue and will allow their characters to disintegrate. This disintegration will usually take the form of a loosening of the moral fibre, which results in timidity of action and slackness in appearance, while those who have gone to seed will be dirty and their appearance will be slovenly. In these latter cases there has been a general loosening of the character due to a partial surrender to fear. The good soldier — the man with high morale — has not surrendered to fear and has maintained his personal standards; the bad soldier — the man with low morale — has become incapable of independent action and has to some extent shed a part of his human individuality.

Morale is a mental and moral quality. It is that which in battle keeps men up on humanity's level. But humanity's level is not enough, because the strongest instinct is the instinct for survival. Morale is also that which develops man's latent heroism so that he will overcome his desire to take the easy way out and surrender to fear. The quality which maintains human dignity in battle and at the same time develops man's heroism is high morale. It is necessary now to make clear what high morale is not. It is not contentment or satisfaction bred from ease or comfort of living. Both of these contain a hint of complacency, an acceptance of luxury as an end in itself. High morale is far more than any of these; for it implies essentially the ability to triumph over discomforts and dangers and carry on with the job.

Nor is high morale achieved through fitness or healthiness alone. It is important not to confuse the idea of physical happiness with morale. The happy faces of men after a good game of football are not necessarily the faces of men with good morale. Morale is a mental rather than a physical quality, a determination to overcome obstacles, an instinct driving a man forward against his own desires. High morale is not happiness. Happiness may be a contributory factor in the maintenance of morale over a long period, but it is no more than that. High morale is not toughness. Some very tough men in war have turned out to be very disappointing in action. Toughness is a physical and not a mental asset. Tough men will occasionally perform an isolated act of bravery. Morale, however, is not a quality which produces a momentary act. It influences behaviour at all times.

In brief, high morale is a quality which is good in itself and is latent in all men. It maintains human dignity. It enables fear and fatigue to be overcome. It is involved with the idea of conscience, but it should not be confused with fitness or happiness or toughness.

Basic Factors of Morale

We must now consider what factors constitute the morale of the soldier in the heat of battle. Certain factors may be described as essential conditions without which high morale cannot exist. These lour basic factors are: (1) leadership, (2) discipline, (3) comradeship, and (4) self-respect. A fifth factor, devotion to a cause, must exist but need not necessarily influence all the soldiers. Finally, there are numerous contributory factors which are of great importance but are not essential conditions.

Leadership

Morale is, in the first place, based on leadership. Good morale is impossible without good leaders. Human beings are fundamentality alike in that certain common characteristics apply to all men in varying degrees. In battle the most important of these characteristics is fear. All men are afraid at one time or another to a greater or lesser extent. In moments of fear they band together and look for guidance; they seek for a person to give decisions; they look for a leader.

In times of war the leader has opportunities denied to him in peace. The difficulties, dangers and discomforts inseparable from the battlefield make men cry out for leadership they can do without in peace. At such moments men are too weak to stand alone; they find the burdens too great to bear and their own selves unequal to the task. The leader himself accepts the burdens of others and by doing so earns their gratitude and the right to lead them. The men recognise in their leader some quality which they themselves do not possess; that quality is "decision". Fear makes men sluggish and indecisive, unable to decide or act for themselves. The leader's power over his men is based on his ability to cut through this "fear paralysis and in so doing to enable others to escape from it. The rightness of the decision taken by the leader is irrelevant. What matters is that the decision should be taken and that the leader should shoulder the responsibility for that decision. The leader must convince his men of its rightness even though he himself may be uncertain of his own judgment. If the leader will decide, the men will follow and will fight. If there is indecision they will hesitate and will flee. In short, "fight and survive", "fear and be slain"; the leader decides.

The leader's power of decision results from his ability to remain imperturbable in the crisis. His greatest asset is the ability to act normally in abnormal conditions, to continue to think rationally when his men have ceased to think, to be decisive in action when they are paralysed by fear. The object of training must be, first, to select those who possess within them the potentialities of leadership, and, secondly, to develop these potentialities. This is accomplished by giving the leader responsibility. A leader's character will develop in proportion to the responsibility with which he has been entrusted. His position as the man responsible for the lives and well-being of his men must be impressed upon him. In battle his preoccupation with his men's affairs will give him less time to think of his own fears. The mere fact of responsibility will increase the leader's powers of decision and make him confident of his ability to handle any crisis. The two vital attributes of a leader are: (a) decision in action, and (b) calmness in crisis. Given these two attributes he will succeed; without them he will fail. Our great problem in peace is to select as leaders men whose brain will remain clear when intensely frightened; the yardstick of "fear" is absent.

Discipline

The object of discipline is the conquest of fear. There are two as-

pects of fear. Fear can suddenly attack a man through his imagination. A corpse in a ditch or a grave by the side of the road will
remind him of his position. He will suddenly realise that he himself is liable to be killed. It is a function of discipline to fortify the
mind so that it becomes reconciled to unpleasant sights and accepts them as normal everyday occurrences. Fear can also creep
upon a man during periods of monotony in the line. At such a time
he will have the opportunity to appreciate the dangers which beset
his life. Fear acting through his thoughts can so reduce the man's
hard core of courage that he will become nervous and fearful. Discipline strengthens the mind so that it becomes impervious to the
corroding influence of fear. It teaches men to confine their thought
within certain definite limits. It instils the habit of self-control.

The basis of fear is the awareness of danger. Man becomes
aware of danger when he feels himself opposed to something more
powerful than himself. It is important for a man to lose his individual feeling and to become an integral part of the battalion, division
and army to which he belongs. It is here that discipline shows its
value, for it can help a man to lose his own identity and become a
part of a larger and stronger unit. It is in this way that discipline
will conquer fear. This corporate sense which discipline creates
helps men to face the unknown.

The method by which the conquest of fear is achieved is the
unifying of men into a group or unit under obedience to orders.
Men require to be united if they are to give of their best. Discipline
seeks to instil into all ranks a sense of unity by compelling them to
obey orders as one man. This obedience to orders is the indispen-
sable condition of good discipline. Men learn to gain confidence
and encouragement from doing the same thing as their fellows;
they derive strength and satisfaction from their company; their
own identities become merged into the larger and stronger identity of their unit. Men must learn to obey orders when all their own
instincts cry out for them not to be obeyed. They must learn to
obey orders in times of stress so that they will do so times of dan-

ger. They must learn to carry out their tasks under any conditions and despite all difficulties. In this way the mass of loose individuals, with their fears and weaknesses, can be welded into a united whole, ready to act on the word of a leader.

Discipline implies a conception of duty. Nothing will be accomplished in the crisis by the man without a sense of duty. The sentry in an outpost holds his ground in the face of an attack because he has a sense of duty to those behind him. This sense is instilled by discipline because it teaches men to obey orders as a matter of course, to know that it is wrong not to obey them, and right — that is, their duty — to do so. For the soldier this conception of duty does not embrace abstractions such as freed.om or empire or democracy. In battle a soldier's sense of duty extends only to the friends who are around him. It is the job of the junior leader to encourage this sense of duty. In brief, discipline seeks to conquer fear by welding men into a cohesive whole, united by obedience to order. It aims to create a body strong enough to carry each of its members through dangers and difficulties which they themselves would be unable to face alone. In this way it promotes comradeship, which is the third factor of morale.

Comradeship

Morale cannot be good unless men come to have affection for each other; a fellow-feeling must grow up which will result in a spirit of comradeship. An army is made of human beings, so that however much a leader may inspire his men, however perfect the discipline, the morale will be hard and unsympathetic if the warmth of the comradeship is not added to it. War, though a hard business, is not necessarily a grim one. Men must laugh and joke together, must enjoy each other's company, and must get fun out of life even in times of danger. Comradeship is based on affection and trust, which between them produce an atmosphere of mutual good will and a feeling of interdependence. Men learn to have faith in each other and to depend on each other according to the abilities of each. Comradeship is a great antidote to fear because it gives a man friends. If he has friends he will derive strength from their presence and will be anxious not to let them down in battle. All men have within them a streak of generosity and unselfishness — a touch of nobility — and these qualities will be brought out in their attitude to their friends. Friendship causes men to give of their best.

In conclusion, comradeship is vital to high morale because it surrounds a man with an atmosphere of warmth and strength at the very moment when he is feeling cold and weak. It encourages his finest instincts, and the demands of friendship serve to strengthen him in battle. These demands are also a challenge to his self-respect — a quality which must now be considered.

Self-Respect

No man can be said to possess high morale if the quality of self-respect is lacking. Soldiers must be encouraged to respect themselves at all times and under all conditions. Self-respect implies a determination to maintain personal standards of behaviour. A man who respects himself will allow neither himself to become slovenly nor his quarters dirty; even in action he will take care to see that his personal appearance suffers as little as possible. It is the job of the non-commissioned officer to maintain this aspect of discipline; it is the function of the officer to encourage and instil self-respect.

Efficiency is inseparable from self-respect. Men must take pride in their ability to carry out all jobs allotted to them. They must feel that they are good soldiers and are therefore of value to other people. Men can be persuaded of this fact by being trusted. A man who feels he is trusted will feel that he is efficient, and he will at once begin to respect himself. He will have confidence in his own ability to fight. Men who are trusted gain self-confidence.

It is the job of the officer to convince his men that he trusts them. Self-respect is a quality which will develop inevitably if the three essential factors already considered are present. It is true to say that without self-respect good morale is impossible; it is equally true to say that if the standards of leadership, discipline and comradeship are high, the quality of self-respect will also be high.

Devotion to a Cause

It is impossible to make devotion to a cause either a basic or a contributory factor to good morale. It must stand by itself between these two categories. I do not believe that soldiers are greatly influenced by "cause"; — they do not advance over dangerous and fire-swept ground in the conscious pursuit of an ideal; they fight for reasons which have little obvious connection with freedom or democracy. There are, of course, exceptions. But rhetorical statements which assert that the soldier

". . . must know what he fights for, And love what he knows"

must not be allowed to confuse the issue. The fact is that the soldier, instead of having "fire in his belly", advances into battle with a cold feeling inside him. These statements must be qualified.

No nation could fight an unpopular war; the war must be accepted by the people, since a democracy cannot oppose the will of the majority of its citizens. The soldier, as a citizen, must therefore be convinced of the rightness of the cause. At least his reaction to the declaration of war must be acquiescence, even if this is only passive : he must not be hostile to it. The way to change this passive acceptance to active enthusiasm in battle has already been given in the four basic factors. Nevertheless, nothing which I have said must be interpreted as minimising the influence of "cause" on those officers and men who are moved by it. For these few, "cause" will be a sustaining and strengthening factor and may be of greater importance to them than any of the four factors.

Contributory Factors

There are certain contributory factors which powerfully assist morale but do not themselves constitute essential conditions for it. It is possible to have high morale without any of these contributory factors, but it is very difficult; it requires the highest standards of leadership and discipline and the strongest feelings of comradeship and self-respect. In the normal case one or more of these contributory factors must be present. There are many of them and only a few are considered here.

Success — High morale is possible in defeat but not during a long period of defeat. On such occasions confidence in the leaders will inevitably wane and the first basis will be undermined. Success will aid good morale by creating confidence in the leader and in the command.

Regimental Tradition — The regimental spirit can be a powerful factor in making for good morale. The more a soldier feels himself to be identified with his regiment the higher will be his morale if the four essential conditions have been fulfilled. There is a difference between comradeship and regimental spirit. Comradeship is the spirit of fellow-feeling which grows up between a small group of men who live and work and fight together. Regimental spirit is the soldier's pride in the traditions of his regiment and his determination to be worthy of them himself. Nothing but good can result from this spirit, which should be constantly encouraged; it is not, however, a basic factor of morale, because in the crisis of battle the majority of men will not derive encouragement from the glories of the past but will seek aid from their leaders and comrades of the present. In other words, most men do not fight well because their ancestors fought well at the Battle of Minden two centuries ago, but because their particular platoon or battalion has good leaders, is well-disciplined, and has developed the feeling of comradeship and self-respect among all ranks on all levels. It is not devotion to some ancient regimental story which steels men in crisis; it is devotion to the comrades who are with them and the leaders who are in front of them.

Personal Happiness — A man should be happy in the sense that his personal life should be in order. Nothing weakens a man more than trouble at home ; it encourages him to think of home, and all that it implies, when he should be occupied with the enemy. It turns his mind to peace and his desire to live at the moment when it is necessary for him to steel himself to face the possibility of death. He must never be allowed to forget that his job is to fight. His function is to kill the enemy and in so doing he must expose himself to danger.

Administration — A man's ordinary day-to-day life must be well organised. Thus, hard conditions imposed on him in training to inculcate discipline do not rule out the desirability of good living quarters; and in the line a soldier's morale will be much improved if the administrative arrangements are good and if he is assured of proper conditions, with a reasonable amount of leisure and comfort when he leaves the front. But here a warning must be given. There is a danger today of "welfare" being considered as an end in itself and not as a means to an end, one of the means of maintaining morale. Welfare by itself will not produce good morale because it is essentially soft; and it has already been stated that morale cannot be good unless it contains a quality of hardness. Hardness and privation are the school of the good soldier; idleness and luxury are his enemies. Men will endure great hardships if they know why and are convinced of the necessity. "Blood, toil, tears and sweat" is not for nothing one of the great rallying calls of the English race. Goering's cry, "Guns before butter", expressed the same truth. If men believe in the need, hardships are in themselves a stimulant to morale. But the opposite is also true. Let there be any suggestion that butter can come before guns and some men will at once choose the butter. If this happens there will be no morale in the sense of this definition.

Propaganda — The uplifting effect of modern propaganda on

a soldier is perhaps a new development. A man's morale is raised immensely by feeling that his efforts are appreciated and applauded, not only by his comrades and officers but by the world at large. Remarkable results can be achieved by the use of modern publicity methods. These results will be achieved only if the fighting soldier is differentiated from the soldier who serves behind the fighting line. The latter often works at dull, monotonous jobs and lacks the stimulus of battle conditions; it is good for his morale that his work should be publicise in the press. But it is no good writing of the Bren gunner and the G.H.Q. clerk in the same terms. The sharp distinction between those who risk their lives in actual battle with the enemy and. those who do not must not be blurred. A fighting soldier thus glorified' will soon become convinced of his own importance. This artificially stimulated feeling of self-importance is a quality lower and less lasting than that of self-respect, but it is none the less of momentary value.

Conclusion

In brief high morale has been defined as the quality which makes men endure and show courage in times of fatigue and danger: The cultivation of morale depends upon the training of leaders, the inculcation, of discipline, the encouragement of comradeship, and the infusing of self-respect. The leaders must have a belief in their cause, and they must pay attention to numerous contributory factors of considerable but secondary importance.

We live today in a scientific age. But we soldiers have to remember that the raw material with which we have to deal is "men". Man is still the first weapon of war. His training is the most important consideration in the fashioning of a fighting army. All modern science is directed towards his assistance but on his efforts depends the outcome of the battle. The morale of the soldier is the most important single factor in war.

Field Marshal The Viscount Montgomery of Alamein

Analysis of Morale in a British Formation

In the half-forgotten defence of Calais in 1940 one British brigade and the elements of one other regiment delayed the advance of an entire wing of the German Army for three days, holding the pressure off Dunkirk and enabling the greater part of the British Expeditionary Force to bring off the miracle of escape to Britain. This was the classic appeal to heroism that a few hold the pass and save the many. The brigade and the fractions of a regiment thus met annihilation in a situation which might have exalted the spirit of any army. Its sacrifice saved the cause of Britain.

But the brigade did this unknowingly. The message from headquarters in London telling it to hold on at all costs because of the high stakes at Dunkirk was never delivered and the men died at their posts believing that their action had almost no meaning in the war. As to the incentive motivating the defenders of Calais, Erik Linklater has written:

"It rather appears that this staunch courage was inspired by obedience to the very fine regimental tradition. Six or eight men in a shell-rocked house full of tawdry French furniture would fight as if they were defending the Holy Sepulchre because the corporal in command has told them, this is where Mr. (Lieutenant) So-and-So said we were to go. And Mr. So-and-So had spoken with the voice of the regiment."

Mr. Linklater comes pretty close to the uttering of a complete truth about esprit. But if I were reconstructing this tale of high courage and seeking the ultimate explanation of why things happened in just the way they did, I would say somewhat less about obedience to the fine regimental tradition and somewhat more about loyalty to Mr. So-and-So and to the corporal who gave his orders.

It is expressing it in too-little terms to say that this pair spoke with the voice of the regiment. In the realest sense they were the regiment in the eyes of the men whom they commanded during the crisis of battle. There can be only one explanation of how the regiment and its fine traditions inspired these men to the extreme point where they were willing to be annihilated in a hopeless battle from which nothing could be saved (as they thought) except the regimental honour; it was because the men who died in the ruins of the shell-rocked house and the debris of the tawdry French furniture had previously discovered the characters of the men who led them.

Colonel Munson, Leadership for American Army Leaders

LEADERSHIP

On Leadership

I would define leadership as:
    "The will to dominate, together with the character which inspires confidence."
    A leader has got to learn to dominate the events which surround him; he must never allow these events to get the better of him; he must allow nothing to divert him from his aim; he must always be on top of his job, and be prepared to accept responsibility.
    We must endeavour to produce, on every level, commanders with these qualities of leadership and character which inspire confidence in others.
    These qualities are probably possessed in some degree by all men chosen as leaders, but they need to be developed by training; and they must be so developed throughout the Army' We must analyse the good and bad points in a man's make-up; we must then develop his good points and teach him to keep the bad points in subjection.

Field Marshal The Viscount Montgomery of Alamein, 'Military Leadership'

Example

As to the way in which some of our Ensigns and lieutenants braved danger — the boys just come out of school — it exceeds all belief. They ran as at cricket!

Wellington, Samuel Roger: Recollections 1859

Looking for Leadership

I am a soldier. In speaking of leadership I do so as a soldier, and when I think about it, as any soldier often must, I do so in the context of battle. Pressures in battle are high and in battle, as a consequence, the problems of leadership stand out in bold relief. But, while battle may be unique, the problems that it exposes are not. For leadership is concerned with getting people to do things and is most keenly needed when difficulties, doubts and dangers are at their greatest. In whatever sphere this is attempted the problems are essentially similar. This is probably why I am speaking now on this programme.

I said that leadership was concerned with getting people to do things. What I meant was getting them "To do things willingly". What then must there be to a leader if he is to secure this willing acceptance of what he wants? He must be able to offer to those under him what they need. First of all they need direction in the execution of a common enterprise. But they have other needs and these of course will vary. It may be courage when they are afraid. It may be perception when they are muddled and confused. He must give them this. But above all, he must be able to take upon himself some part of their trouble and so help to secure their release from a burden which can be intolerable. He must be the possessor of qualities which are relevant to the task with which his men are concerned, skills and qualities which they respect. Even at the lowest level of military leadership the leader may not have all the relevant skills. It does not matter: what the group wants is a leader not a paragon.

He must have understanding. It is worth remembering that militant practice is group practice. Many of the military forms which look so unnecessary or even absurd — the worship of regimental totems, the eccentricities of dress and custom, the cultivation of a separate identity for the group — these have been developed and are still dedicated precisely to the creation and maintenance of that coherence on which the effective performance of a group under pressure depends. The leader must realise this.

He must be able to manage fear, first in himself for if he cannot then his leadership must begin to fail: but in others also for otherwise they may collapse. He must also be able to manage failure as well as success, for failure is seldom final and the man helped on from one failure may well fail no more.

The personal qualities required are not found everywhere. A few people are born with them but too few, for the Army as for any other enterprise where leadership is wanted. Men who might be leaders have therefore to be sought out, and then trained and helped to form the habit of acting as the leader should.

I would add only this. A man really only gets a full response from the men he leads by something approaching a complete fusion of his own identify with the whole that he and they together form. This demands a great deal of the leader: it is as well to remember that it can also be hard on the men he leads. For he may move on to other groups, perhaps larger ones, to identify as fully with the new group as with the old. Those remaining in the old one may be left hurt and lost. The parting of leader and led is at some time bound to happen and can be painful unless it is handled with a high degree of imagination. This is not always found.

In short, successful military leadership is impossible without the leader's total engagement in the task in hand and to the group committed to his care for its discharge. For all I know, this may be so not only in the military, but in other spheres as well.

General Sir John Hackett: Transcript of his broadcast 'Looking for Leadership' February 1968

Enlightened Leadership

"War is pre-eminently the art of the man who dares to take the risk; of the man who thinks deeply and clearly; of the man who, when accident intervenes, is not thereby cast down, but changes his plans and disposition with the readiness of a resolute and reflective mind, which so far as is possible has foreseen and provided against difficulties."

This quotation gives a short word-picture of the qualifications for leadership, a vital factor in war.

The peoples of the British commonwealth of Nations pride themselves on instinctive powers of leadership, and history has shown that this pride is well founded, but natural leadership by itself is not enough for modern war, which demands and exacts the highest standard of military knowledge and tactical ability; clear thinking, cool judgment and initiative; spied and decision in action; physical courage endurance and resolution; clear and sympathetic understanding of human nature, loyalty and unselfishness and constant forethought.

The first essential in a leader is that he should have the complete confidence of all those under his command. Now, no man can inspire confidence in others who is not confident in himself, and self-confidence comes from knowledge. A thorough understanding of modern weapons and organisation, tactics and the details of administration affecting all those under his command must therefore be acquired by every leader. He must show his troops that he can plan soundly, lead resolutely and deal promptly and effectively with the unexpected. In addition, to gain the full confidence of his troops, a leader must have their personal friendship and trust. He must study them individually, understand their feelings and appreciate their capabilities and limitations. He must always give first consideration to their welfare and interests. The true leader must be able to enlist the willing co-operation of his men. Mutual trust and comradeship must form the basis of the relationship between leaders and their men.

Leaders must study the enemy as well as their own troops so that they can take full advantage of weaknesses in the enemy's character and methods. They must be adept at devising ways and means: of deceiving the enemy to gain surprise. Deep thought is essential in the analysis of any military problem. The object to be achieved must first be decided and then must be clearly stamped on the leader's mind. It must never be lost sight of. All the factors bearing on the problem in hand must be carefully considered. No matter what his task, every leader must make a logical appreciation of each particular problem in order to decide his plan. Any other form of approach will result in important factors being overlooked, and will lead to false conclusions and an unsound plan. Forethought is needed to provide for the unexpected, and to ensure that no opportunities are lost. The leader must always be several steps ahead of events in his mind. At the same time he must face realities, and. refrain from any tendency towards wishful thinking. He must be prepared to take risks without being foolhardy.

Having made his plan, a leader must make his intention, and the method whereby he proposes to carry it out, perfectly clear to all those taking part. Plans must be cleverly designed, but not complicated, relate to realities, and adaptable to changing situations. Above all, they must cater for surprise and the greatest possible concentration of effort and resources at the decisive point. The leader must decide where that point is only so will he be able to retain the initiative.

The leader next has to face the most difficult problem of all — how to control his troops throughout the battle, how to adjust their action to rapidly changing situations to ensure that the enemy's counter-efforts are fruitless, and that no opportunities are lost. From the section leader, who controls his men by word of mouth, to the commander-in-chief, who depends on long-range wireless communications and flying visits to his subordinates, all leaders must exercise their personal influence on the course of the battle. They must impress their will on all those under their command, otherwise the battle will take charge of itself, initiative will be lost, reserves will be frittered away, and chances will be missed.

Control in battle is a question of communications in relation to time. The system to be adopted must be carefully thought out beforehand to ensure that not a second is lost in collecting information or in giving orders for action. Leaders must constantly practice exercising control under varying conditions of battle. They must always be thinking of ways and means by which they can accelerate and improve their system.

Success will depend upon the personal resolution and endurance of leaders and their troops. Leaders must inspire their troops with the will to win, an indomitable determination to defeat the enemy, and to endure every form of hardship and danger to achieve success. By his own energy and confidence, by personal example, undaunted courage and determination, a leader must lift his men to that supreme effort that gives final victory in a hard-fought battle. He must show them that, even when endurance appears to have been exhausted, another effort is still possible, while remembering that every effort cannot be supreme.

Throughout an action leaders must constantly review the tactical situation making fresh appreciations in the light of events. Speed of thought, decision, and action are essential. Leaders must use their initiative, governing their action by their knowledge of their commander's intention, and his general plan. Every opportunity for action in furtherance of the general plan must be seized at once without waiting for orders. Whatever the situation, inaction will always be wrong.

Leaders must be on their guard against becoming unduly elated by success or depressed by failure. They must never take counsel of their fears. There are no hopeless situations, only hopeless men. When things look bad and difficulties loom large, consideration of the enemy's problems will be the best tonic. Leaders must be cheerful, reasoned optimists. Depression and gloom achieve nothing and may well have a disastrous effect on the spirits of others. When success has been achieved leaders must not pause, but must exploit it to the full. No relaxation of effort can be allowed until the enemy has been finally destroyed.

After an engagement a leader's first thought and action must be for the welfare of his troops; his own comfort and rest must come last.

Loyalty is an essential quality in a leader; it must extend to his subordinates as well as to his superiors. A leader must never take shelter behind the shortcomings or mistakes of his subordinates. When plans for which he is responsible go wrong he must take the blame, correcting the mistakes of his subordinates himself. Every leader has the right to express his views to his superiors on any question under consideration, but once a decision has been reached he must support it loyally with every means in his power, and put an immediate stop to any criticisms.

Jealousy, resentment and self-seeking are human failings which leaders must prevent by fair dealing and suppress when they arise. Nothing is more harmful to success in war than friction between leaders. It is unpardonable.

Discipline is the basis of all military effort. The highest standard is needed to stand the test of war. A leader must discipline himself before he can expect to maintain that high standard of discipline required in all those under his command.

Finally, the strain and speed of modern war demands the highest standard of physical fitness in all troops; nerves must be steeled as well. Leaders have the greatest strain to bear and must be the fittest of all.

A short guide to leadership is given as follows:

Perfect your military knowledge, study the use of weapons, their tactical handling, the enemy's character and methods, and way to make use of ground.

Study the men under your command. Know them well and be

known to them. Gain their confidence by your knowledge, energy and skill, and by your interest in their welfare. Always be cheerful with them, however you may feel. Teach yourself to think out reasoned appreciations leading to clever but uncomplicated plans quickly but unhurriedly.

Study methods of deception and make full use of them. Always aim at misleading the enemy. Always seek surprise. Keep your object clearly before you. Concentrate your efforts and resources at the decisive point. Always think well ahead.

Work out the best methods of control in different tactical situations. Practise them constantly.

Study the situation carefully. Don't waste any time. Make up your mind and stick to it. Get out your orders quickly. Make certain that everyone clearly knows what you intend to be done.

Maintain the initiative. Make opportunities and seize them at once. Don't wait for them to come. Be prepared to take risks, but don't be foolhardy. Know your commander's intention and act in accordance with it. Don't wait for orders. Inaction is always wrong.

Never take counsel of your fears. Think of the enemy's difficulties and how you can take advantage of them. Remember that it is will-power that wins. Never relax your efforts until victory is won. Attend to the comfort of the troops before you think of your own.

Be loyal to your superiors and to your subordinates. Express your views clearly and frankly, but when a decision has been reached support it fully, and stop all criticism. Never take shelter behind others when things for which you are responsible have gone wrong.

Refrain from jealousy, resentment and self-seeking. Be tactful. Never make friction. Be thoughtful and considerate, but maintain firm discipline. Never order troops to do what you are not prepared to do yourself. Never give an unnecessary order. Never overlook failure to carry one out.

Keep fit yourself and make certain that your men do, too. Keep your own nerves under control and study your men's.

Last of all, remember that success in war depends more than anything else on the will to win.

Brigadier Maunsell, an extract from The R.M.A. Sandhurst study, Morale, Leadership, Discipline.

Being Straight

"There is one trait in the character of a leader that above all things really counts, and it perhaps counts in war even more than in peace. Being straight. No amount of ability, knowledge, or cunning, can ever make up for not being straight. Once those under him find out that a commander is absolutely straight in all his dealings with them, and free from the slightest trait of self-interest, other than the self-interest of which we are all guilty when striving for the victory of causes we believe to be right, they will love him as their leader, trust him, work for him, follow him — and should occasion arise die for him, with the fundamental ability of the British soldier which comes to the surface when things are at their worst."

"Basilisk" Talks on Leadership

Old Nosey

The sight of his long nose among us on a battle ten thousand men, any day of the week.

Captain John Kincaid, quoted in Britain at Arms compiled by Thomas Gilby

Where's Arthur?

A comrade of his, tells Cooper also, as they were beginning the fight, called out: "Where's Arthur?" He meant Wellington. The answer was given: "I don't know — I don't see him !" Rejoined the first private: "Aw wish he wur here !" "So did I", comments Sergeant Cooper.

Edward Fraser, The Soldiers Whom Wellington Led

Leadership

I have been asked by your Commandant to talk to you about Leadership. It is a difficult subject to define, and difficult also to discuss in detail, because it involves the discussion of many things that we, the British, do not often like talking about moral, spiritual and emotional factors that it does not come very easy to us to discuss in public; but it is so vitally important that I think that we have all got to accept the disadvantage of talking about these matters.

There are some people who believe that leadership is something which is inborn, or which you acquire automatically at a public school; but neither of those things is true. There are certain fundamental qualities which affect leadership and which depend to a very large extent on upbringing and the moral and spiritual values which you learn in your family and in your environment as a young man; but there is no special way, nor is there any special caste or class, which has the prerogative of leadership.

There are many forms of leadership. Political parties have their leaders; every big organisation in industry or commerce, all have their leaders; and, at the other end of the scale, so do dance bands, and so do gangs of thieves and smugglers. There are many qualities that apply equally to every type of leader, but you and I are concerned with one particular type of leadership — to my mind the highest type of all – and that is leadership on the battlefield; and I believe it to be of the highest type because it has to be exercised under conditions of great difficulty and considerable danger. I would like you to be quite clear about the conditions under which you will have to exercise leadership. You will frequently be tired. You may also be cold and wet, and hungry, and thirsty. You may be dripping with sweat, or you may be freezing with cold. You won't know precisely what is going on; you won't know exactly where the enemy is; you certainly won't know what he is going to do, or what his capabilities are of doing anything. You may not know where your own people are, or what they are going to do. To put it briefly, you have got to be able to exercise leadership in conditions of fatigue and fear, uncertainty and ignorance, and often in isolation. That is what makes it extremely difficult, and that is why leadership on the battlefield calls, in my view, for the highest qualities.

Now, you have got a good deal to help you. You have got the comradeship of your men and, I hope their confidence; you have the traditions and the reputation of the Regiment or Corps to which you have the honour to belong; and, above all, you have the knowledge that what you have to do, however difficult and dangerous it may be, you are doing as your duty in the service of your Queen and your country, and even above that you have the knowledge of your duty to God. So that you have many beliefs and factors to help you in this particularly difficult job, and it is always as well to remember that when you talk about the difficulties.

Many qualities are required in a leader. Different people have different views about which are the more important. In my opinion there are five outstanding — mental and physical, moral and spiritual qualities without which you cannot hope to be successful and a good leader on the battlefield. The first of those qualities is a mental and physical one, and that is fitness — absolute fitness of mind and body. If your brain is not clear, you cannot control it and make it think logically and quickly and come to sound conclusions: then you cannot make the plans or the decisions that are required of a leader of men in battle. If your body is not absolutely fit so that you can force out of it that last ounce of effort that is needed to carry through your job, or to achieve success — well, you won't succeed. So absolute fitness of mind and body essential.

Then I would say that you have got to have complete integrity. You have got to be honest, not only with yourselves but with the men you lead and the people with whom you work; and honesty and integrity are things that you cannot compromise with — you cannot alter; if you do, you will lose confidence and you will not be able to lead. You must have complete integrity.

Next after that — not in any order of priority, but this is how I have put them down to keep them in my own mind — there is an enduring courage. Pretty well everyone can be brave for a few minutes. Most of us can, if we steel ourselves to it, take one plunge, or make one decision, or incur one risk. But the sort of courage you must have to lead on the battlefield is an enduring courage, and one that will go on when other people falter; one that will enable you to do what you know to be right, irrespective of the danger or the difficulty, often contrary to the advice of well-meaning friends. That is the kind of courage which men who aspire to lead on the battlefield have got to produce — an enduring courage.

Then you must have daring initiative. Initiative means doing right away what you might, if you had time, think of doing a few minutes later. If you wait for things to happen to you, they will happen all right — and here I am quoting the words of my predecessor, also spoken here: they will happen to you, but they won't be what you like, and they certainly won t bring you success. Initiative means seeing at once — and very quickly — what needs to be done, making up your mind to do it, and then seeing it through right to the bitter end. When it is a choice between two courses, one cautious and one bold and daring, well then, to gain success, take the bold and daring course. The quality required, therefore, is one of daring initiative.

Then you must have undaunted will-power. The will-power is the motive power; it is what enables you to make yourself fit in mind and body; to produce in you — in your heart — the courage, the enduring courage that I spoke of; to give you the courage to do your duty and to make the sacrifice that may be called from you. It is the will-power that forces you to take the initiative, to make the plan, to do what is required, and to see it through: and that will-power must be "undaunted", it must never allow itself to be overcome or subdued. Perhaps the finest example living today of the power and influence for good of a man with undaunted will-power is our Prime Minister. In one of the critical periods of the last war he spoke certain words I am going to quote to you now. He said: "All the great struggles in history have been won by superior will-power wresting victory in the teeth of odds, or upon the narrowest of margins." It is the will-power that is superior, that can wrest victory in the teeth of odds — that is the type of will-power that has got to be developed in a leader on the battlefield.

Now I would like you to notice not only the qualities that I have mentioned, but the adjectives I have applied to them, because in those adjectives are implied a great many of the other qualities. I spoke of "absolute" finest, of "complete" integrity, of "enduring" courage, of "bold, daring initiative", and of "undaunted" will-power; and there is a great deal of meaning in the adjectives as well as in the nouns which I would like you to remember. Those are five outstanding qualities that are essential, in my opinion, as a leader.

There are other requirements that are needed as well. There are many of them, but there are three that I would like to mention to you here this afternoon. The first is knowledge. If you are to have the courage to take the initiative, to produce the will-power that is needed' you must have knowledge. You must know more than those under your command — a good deal more. You must know the power and the capabilities of the weapons at your disposal. You must know how the other resources that you can rely on to help you can best be used. You must know how much you can ask of your men. You must know what the enemy's capabilities are. You must know how best all arms can co-operate and combine to gain success on the battlefield. You must knowhow to use the ground and any other aids there may be. You must know what support you can count on from the air and other supporting weapons. All that requires a great deal of study and thought, and practice and experience.

You are learning here — learning about many things other than the ones I have spoken of, and they all have an important bearing on your future career as officers. The point that I would like to make to you now is that you do not complete your learning here; you go on, and you go on ail through your service, learning by study, by thought, by practice and experience, and unless you do you will never reach the standard of leadership at the various levels of rank which you may hold — you will never reach that standard. So go on learning all the time. Remember that knowledge is the basis of skill, and that skill is the basis of success.

The next quality that I wish to mention is judgment. You have got to have judgment. You have got to be able to assess values, and assess them quickly and under difficult circumstances, and that calls for judgment, and judgment is only learned by experience and practice. You will never learn to judge and to assess value if you are afraid of making mistakes — never. So don't be afraid of making mistakes. Don't be afraid of errors of judgment. You will have them all right. They come to all of us. They come pretty frequently to me. If you are afraid of them, if you are afraid to face them, you will never gain the experience that is needed to enable you to use your judgment properly and fully. So remember that you have got to learn to judge: you have got to learn to weigh up priorities — that modern word — all through your service, and you can only do so by judging the value of this and that and the other; by developing your judgment and your sense of values you will find the principles of war are frequently in conflict — in any particular problem with which you may be faced, and you have to weigh up and decide which in the particular circumstances is the more important of the principles — which you can stick to, which you can discard — and that needs judgment. That judgment only comes from knowledge, practice and experience.

The third thing I would like to mention this afternoon is the team spirit, because you cannot get success on the battlefield by yourself; you have got to work with other people. You have got, in the first place, to get the full confidence of the men under your command; you have got to train them to work as a team, and you have got to lead them as a team leader. Then your team has to fit in with other teams, and so on all the way up, and throughout the whole business of life, and training, and war. The Army — throughout every part of it — has got to work as a number of teams, and these teams have got to work together to one common end, and so the team spirit becomes of supreme importance: and it is only as a member — as a leader — of a well-trained, confident, highly skilled team that you can exercise successful leadership on the battlefield.

Success in battle really comes from a combination of the skill and daring of the leader and the skill and confidence of the led, and we, the British, nation, have produced in the past many great and splendid leaders. The one that is outstanding in my mind as an example of what I have been trying to say to you this afternoon in regard to skill and daring and confidence is Nelson. You will wonder why I have quoted a sailor to an audience of soldiers, but it doesn't matter what service he comes from — the three Services have got to work together. If you study Nelson's battles you will see that in every case he gained his victory by his skill, his knowledge, his boldness, and by the confidence that everyone who served under him had in his judgment and in his decisions: and that is the standard at which we have all got to aim to obtain victory in battle.

There is one other thing that I would like to say to you: At British officers, you will never have all you want, all you need. You will be short of this, or that, or the other. Sometimes you will be short of men; at other times your equipment or weapons may not be as good as you think they ought to be, nor will you have as many as you would like. You may be short of ammunition. You may also be short of food and water, or other necessary things. When these circumstances arise — as they will do often throughout your service, both in peace and war — there is only one motto, and that is to make certain that you do the very best you can with what you have got. Don't bellyache about what you have not got, but get on and make certain that you do your utmost with what you have got. It is very important for British officers, in whatever arm or branch of the Service they may be, to make up their minds that that is what they will always do: and that is what I hope all of you here will always make your motto in the years to come.

Now, to sum up what I have tried to say to you this afternoon, I would like to put it like this. First, keep fit — absolutely fit. Then, be honest — honest with yourselves and honest with all those with whom you work. Then, have courage — and make it an enduring courage. Next, be bold, be daring, and when there is a choice take the bold and daring course. Make the very most always of what you have got. And never, never never give in.

Field-Marshal The Lord Harding of Petherton, addressing the Senior Division in July 1953, when C.I.G.S.

The Good Commander

When on active service the commander must prove himself conspicuously careful in the matter of forage, quarters, water-supply, outposts, and all other requisites; forecasting the future and keeping ever a wakeful eye in the interest of those under him; and in case of any advantage won, the truest gain which the head of affairs can reap is to share with his men the profits of success.

Indeed, to put the matter in a nutshell, there is small risk a general will be regarded with contempt by those he leads, if, whatever he may have to preach, he shows himself best able to perform. If, further, the men shall see in their commander, one who, with the knowledge how to act, has force of will and cunning to make them get the better of the enemy; and, if, further, they have the notion well into their heads that this same leader may be trusted not to lead them recklessly against the foe, without the help of Heaven, or despite the auspices — I say, you have a list of virtues which make those under his command the more obedient to their ruler.

Xenophon, written about the beginning of the 4th Century B.C.

Advance

Brigadier Rowe had proceeded within thirty paces of the pales about Blenheim before the enemy gave their first fire, by which a great many brave officers and soldiers fell, but that did not discourage their gallant commander from marching directly up to the very pales, on which he struck his sword before he suffered a man to fire.

Dr. Hare's Journal, quoted in Britain at Arms

Before Agincourt

What's he that wishes so?
My cousin Westmoreland ? No, my fair cousin:
If we are marked to die, we are now
To do our country loss: and if to live,
The fewer men, the greater share of honour.
God's will, I pray thee wish not one man more.
By jove, I am not covetous for gold,
Nor care I who doth feed upon my cost:
It yearns me not if men my garments wear:
Such outward things dwell not in my desires'
But if it be a sin to covet honour,
I am the most offending soul alive.
No, faith, my coz, wish not a man from England:
God's peace, I would not lose so great an honour,
As one man more, methinks, would share from me,
For the best hope I have. O, do not wish one more:
Rather proclaim it, Westmoreland, through my host,
That he which hath no stomach to this fight,
Let him depart, his passport shall be made,
And crowns for convoy put into his purse:
We would not die in that man's company,
That fears his fellowship, to die with us'
This day is called the feast of Crispian:—
He that outlives this day, and comes safe home,
Will stand a tip-toe when this day is named,
And rouse him at the name of Crispian'
He that shall see this day, and live old age,
Will yearly on the vigil feast his neighbours.
And say, "Tomorrow is Saint Crispian."
Then will he strip his sleeve, and show' his scars.
And say, "These wounds I had on Crispian's day."'

Old men forget; yet all shall be forgot,
But he'll remember, with advantages,
What feats he did that day. Then shall our names,
Familiar in his mouth as household words,
Harry the king, Bedford and Exeter,
Warwick and Talbot, Salisbury and Gloucester,
Be in their flowing cups freshly remembered.
This story shall the good man teach his son;
And Crispin Crispian shall ne'er go by,
From this day to the ending of the world,
But we in it shall be remembered;
We few, we happy few, we band of brothers,
For he today that sheds his blood with me
Shall be my brother: be he ne'er so vile,
This day shall gentle his condition.
And gentlemen in England, now a-bed,
Shall think themselves accursed they were not here:
And hold their manhoods cheap, whiles any speaks
That fought with us upon Saint Crispian's day.

Shakespeare, King Henry V's speech before Agincourt

Simple Maths

"Ten good soldiers wisely led
Will beat a hundred without a head."

Euripides

DISCIPLINE

Discipline

Discipline is teaching which makes a man do something which he would not, unless he had learnt that it was the right, the proper, and the expedient thing to do. At its best, it is instilled and maintained by pride in oneself, in one's unit, in one's profession; only at its worst by a fear of punishment.

Field-Marshal Earl Wavell, *The Good Soldier*

On Discipline

The basis of this training must be self-discipline. A man must learn to be master of himself and to keep in subjection the bad qualities in his make-up. Self-discipline can be developed by training in such things as conception of duty, self-control, self-respect, endurance, and so on. We then have collective discipline and there is no doubt that the initial training in this subject is best carried out by drill. Men must betaught instinctively to obey orders, whatever they are. I do not believe men wilt fight voluntarily for a cause without the iron bonds of discipline. The best form of discipline is the subordination of self for the benefit of the community.

Discipline is the backbone of the efficiency of an army; no changes in methods of warfare or in scientific developments will affect this truth. Discipline in the soldier becomes loyalty in the officer. I would like to give you my general views on the subject of discipline. It is important that our young officers should think rightly on this vital subject, since discipline is the essence of an army.

The word "discipline" has a somewhat nasty smell to some people. I do not think that is right. Possibly many people do not understand what is meant by it. I believe that the idea of discipline, properly understood, underlies civilian life in the same way as it is the basis of military life. In other words, discipline is both a civilian and a military necessity.

The basis of all discipline is self-discipline. This self-discipline may come from within a person, or it may be imposed upon him from without. Whatever its source, it involves the idea of sell-control and self-restraint. This conception of self-restraint underlies the whole of Christian teaching on personal conduct, and it is impressed on every child from nursery days onwards. Obedience to the Ten Commandments means that we submit ourselves to the necessary self-discipline to enable ourselves to carry them out. I maintain that discipline has a moral foundation, and none of us need be afraid to admit it.

Discipline has also what I call, for lack of a better word, a social basis. All civilised communities demand a degree of self-control from their people. In the interests of the community as a whole, each of us willingly submits to the supremacy of the law, and the authority of its agents, the police. We all recognise that the interests of the community as a whole make demands on us as individuals and, in order that all of us may live happily and freely together, we voluntarily impose upon ourselves a certain restraint.

In Britain we believe in a subordination of self for the benefit of the community. This involves a voluntary self-discipline which recognises and respects the rights of others, and, in so doing, enables us all to enjoy freedom of thought and speech. And at the same time we believe in a state which, recognising the importance of the individual, only imposes those restraints upon him which are necessary for the communal good.

Therefore discipline has both a moral and a social foundation. There can be no doubt of its military significance. It is the backbone of an army, and no changes in methods of warfare, or in scientific developments, will affect this truth.

Therefore, the youth of today must receive discipline training. How is this done?

All of us have in our make-up good points and bad points. Training in self-discipline consists in analysing a man's character and then in developing the good points whilst teaching him to hold in subjection the bad points. This leads on, automatically, to collective discipline, in which the outstanding factor is the subordination of self for the benefit of the community. We must work on these lines in the Army.

Field-Marshal The Viscount Montgomery of Alamein

Natural Discipline

Foreign visitors sometimes talk of our 'natural' discipline. Of course it is not natural ! You might as well talk of the 'instincts of a gentleman'. A man becomes a gentleman only by overcoming his instincts. It is the same with discipline.

Field-Marshal Sir William Slim, Courage and Other Broadcasts

Enlightened Discipline - Trafalgar 1805

Consciously or unconsciously. Nelson in those last weeks off Cadiz was fashioning a tradition and a legend that was to be of a priceless service to England. He reminded the Navy that, whatever the bonds of authority, leadership was not a mere matter of transmitting orders but of evoking the will to serve. Building on all that was best in the great naval tradition in which he had been nurtured and discarding all that was bad, he established an ideal of discipline that was as revolutionary an advance on the dead, unfeeling authoritarianism of the past as the teachings of Rousseau, and far more practical. It was founded, not on a corporate abstraction, but on the individual who alone, as he saw, embodied the principle of life. It's ideal was liberty in a framework of discipline — a liberty that worked and was grafted, in the English mode, on nature. Captain Fremantle testified how pleasant it was, after Lord Nelson's arrival, to be given constant change of scene and occupation, freedom of choice and method, yet to know precisely how far one might go.

It was this which, as an officer said, double-manned every ship in the line. Nelson was essentially a humanitarian who, wooing men to duty, trusted them and had the imagination to see into their hearts. By his reckoning, the best disciplinarian was he who most loved and understood men, who remembered that they were human beings and treated them accordingly. One of his first acts was to order that the names and families of all killed and wounded should be reported to him for transmission to the Chairman of the Patriotic Fund and that an account of every man's case should accompany him to hospital. In this spirit he allowed Sir Robert Calder to return in his own flag-ship to England to face his court martial, thus depriving the Fleet of one of its precious three-deckers at the very moment that he was fretting for every gun to annihilate the enemy. "I much fear I shall incur the censure of the Board," he wrote to the Admiralty, "but I trust that I shall be considered to have done right as a man to a brother officer in affliction — my heart could not stand it". It would have been idle for authority to complain; such tenderness and consideration were an essential part of Nelson's success. He could not discard them without ceasing to be Nelson.

Sir Arthur Bryant, Years of Victory

Duty and Discipline

To obey God's orders as delivered by conscience — that is duty; to obey man's orders as issued by rightful authority — that is discipline. The foundation of both alike is denial of self for a higher good. Unless the lesson of duty be first well learned, the lesson of discipline can be but imperfectly understood.

Sir John Fortescue, A Gallant Company

Obedience and Discipline

I come now to that which can be inspired only by the soldier, the unity, artificial but incomparably strong, which is bound up with the name of discipline. Military discipline — how some people, loathe and others worship it; and how little the majority of both have really thought about it! What is its principle? The organised abnegation of the individual self in favour of the corporate self. What is its object? That tens of thousands may act together as one under the guidance of a single will. What are its methods? Immediate and unquestioning obedience to superior command. Immediate and unquestioning obedience — that is what is the stumbling block, the skandalon to so many. There are of course a certain number of people who can obey no one, but must always be a law — and an exceedingly erratic law unto themselves. The name of the poet Shelley will probably occur to some of you, but I am not thinking of such as Shelley. I have in my mind rather those excellent but generally unthinking persons who shrink with horror from the idea of a man's abdicating his civil rights. 'What', they say, 'a man must obey even an unjust command, under pain it may be of death! It is monstrous!' For purposes of civil life it might be monstrous, but not for purposes of implicit obedience, which is the thing that matters in an Army. Let there be justice as far as possible by all means; but, as a general principle, it is better for an army that an injustice should be done than that an order should be disobeyed. This, however, is an argument that cannot appeal to our imaginary objector, because he has read no military history."

Sir John Fortescue, *Military History*, Lectures delivered at Trinity College, Cambridge

Liberty implies Discipline

If you get up from that chair you are sitting in and take out your car or bicycle, you can choose where you want to go, your own destination. That's liberty! But, as you drive or ride through the streets towards it, you will keep to the left of the road. That's discipline! You will keep to the left without thinking very much about it, but if you do think for a moment, you will find that there is a connection between liberty and discipline.

First of all, you will keep to the left for your own advantage. If you insist on liberty to drive on any side of the road you fancy, you will end up, not where you want to be, but on a stretcher. And there's not much liberty about that! So you accept discipline, because you know that in the long run it is the only way in which you can get to where you want to go quickly and safely.

Other people have as much right to go where they want to as you have. If you career all over the road you will get in their way, delay them, and put them in danger. So for their sakes as well as your own you keep to the left.

But it will be no use your keeping to the left if others on the road don't do the same. You will expect them to. You will trust to their common sense. You will rely on their discipline.

Lastly, even supposing you are tempted to go scooting about

on the wrong side, you probably won't. At the back of your mind will be the thought "If I do the police will be after me". In the last resort there must be some force which can punish disobedience to the law.

There are thus four reasons why you keep to the left:

(i) Your own advantage.

(ii) Consideration for others.

(iii) Confidence in your fellows, and

(iv) Fear of punishment.

Whenever we put a curb on our natural desire to do as we like, whenever we temper liberty with discipline, we do so for one or more of those reasons. It is relative weight we give to each of these reasons that decides what sort of discipline we have. And that can vary from the pure self-discipline of the Sermon on the Mount to the discipline of the concentration camp — the enforced discipline of fear.

Field-Marshal Sir William Slim, Courage and Other Broadcasts

THE BRITISH SOLDIER

The Soldier

". . . To dare boldly,
In a fair cause, and for their country's safety:
To run upon the cannon's mouth undaunted;
To obey their leaders, and shun mutinies;
To bear with patience the winter's cold
And summer's scorching heat, and not to faint
When plenty of provision fails, with hunger,
Are the essential parts that make up a soldier."

Philip Massinger, (1583-1640)

The Mark of Greatness

This is the last in a series of broadcasts called "The Mark of Greatness." In the preceding talks, well-known people have described, each in their own walk of life, a man whom he had known and judged to be great. I did the same.

As a soldier, I have been asked to say something about the greatest soldier I have met and known. So I'm going to. The funny thing is, I can't tell you his name. It changes. Sometimes he has got an English name, sometimes Scottish, sometimes Welsh or Irish. That's because the soldier I want to talk about, the greatest soldier I have met — and, believe me, I have met a lot of all sorts — is the ordinary British soldier.

I hope you don't think it's a foul to choose as my Great Man, not a single hero, but a whole group of men. Our race and our Army have produced great men enough. We have had our Pitts and our Churchills, our Marlboroughs and our Wavells, but I believe their greatness, in their finest hours, was that they expressed and focused the spirit and the qualities that infused the whole British people.

Any nation, now and then, may throw up a great man but, unless its people have greatness in them, it will not cut a very noble figure at the bar of history. An Army must have Generals to lead it, but if the only men in it who have the Mark of Greatness are the Generals, it will win few victories.

To be a great man — or a people — must pass two tests. They must show greatness in character and greatness in achievement. Now there are whole sections of our people, luckily for us large sections, which have shown in a special degree those marks of greatness.

There are our ordinary British housewives. If you want to know what greatness of character is, look at them in the blitz; if you want to know greatness of achievement look now at the children they raised in hardship and peril. But I have to deal with someone else — great also in character and achievement — the British soldier. Think for a moment of the soldier's job. In war he has not only to fight but, in order to be able to fight, he has continually to perform every activity that goes on in a civilian community, and do it under the most uncomfortable, nerve-racking, and dangerous conditions. In peace he is often called upon to restore order or carry on essential services when these tasks have proved too difficult for the civil authorities.

What qualities does he need for all this? He must have courage, lots of it; endurance, moral and physical; skill with his weapons and at the techniques of his trade — for soldiering these days is a highly skilled trade. He must be adaptable and he must have discipline.

A formidable list that — but if he fails in one of them he cannot be a good — let alone a great — soldier.

As to courage, our race, whatever its faults, has never failed for want of courage. From the days of Joan of Arc down to the British soldier today, our friends and, what's perhaps more to the point, our enemies have picked out the British soldier as the staunchest of comrades and most formidable of foes.

It is not that the British soldier is braver than other soldiers. He is not — but he is brave for a bit longer, and it's that bit that counts. Endurance is the very fibre of his courage and of his character. He stays where he is until he has won. He did it at Gibraltar two hundred years ago; a few years back he was doing it at Kohima. He has done it since.

Many years ago, when I was a young officer, my battalion was hard pressed and I was sent with a couple of men to get in touch with a unit which we hoped was still on our left. Worming our way from one bit of cover to the next, we eventually dropped into a trench that had been badly smashed by shellfire. Pistol in hand, I scrambled over the fallen earth, through bay after bay, finding nothing but wreckage and the dead. I think I would have turned back then, but I was as frightened to go back as to go on. So I went on. At last, round a traverse I heard voices. My heart in my mouth, I strained my ears to listen. An agitated voice was proclaiming that another attack was coming and they'd all be wiped out. There was a pause and then one of those creamy West Country voices drawled, "Aw, don' 'ee worry. Us'n'll beat they!" I'd found the Glosters.

The British soldier in his long career has suffered so many disasters, won so many victories, that neither the one nor the other unduly depresses or elates him. Come what may, he holds to his inflexible confidence in ultimate victory. It may take a long time, it may mean all sorts of grim things, but "Us'n'll beat they!"

Unlike most others, the British Army has to be ready to fight or serve anywhere. Western Europe or farthest Asia, desert or jungle, it's all in the day's work. A few hundred years of that have bred in the British soldier an adaptability to climate, terrain and conditions that is one of his most valuable assets.

In the same way, he readily adopts new weapons. The Britisher fights best when he can see his enemy — and that's why, I think, his skill has always been high with his personal short-range weapons. He first gained international fame as a bowman, whose hard-driven shafts broke the armoured chivalry of France. The parade ground volleys of Minden; the deadly disciplined musketry of the thin red line of the Peninsula; the steady fifteen-rounds-a-minute of the old contemptibles; down to the anti-tank gunners of the desert still firing as Panzers ground over them, held this tradition of skill at arms. May we always keep it, for it is the foundation of battle craft.

Any Army without discipline is no more than a mob, alternating between frightened sheep and beasts of prey. Discipline, as the British soldier has demonstrated it in peace and war, is the old Christian virtue of unselfishness, of standing by your neighbour, your comrade. It is the sacrifice of a man's comfort, inclination, safety, even life, for others, for something greater than himself. It is the refusal to be the weak link in the chain that snaps under strain.

Once, from the safety of a well-dug command post, I looked down on a battery of artillery in action in the African bush. It was firing at five rounds per gun per minute and, idly I timed the nearest gun. In that area the enemy, unfortunately, had complete local air supremacy, and guns, unless engaged in some vital task, were ordered to remain silent whenever hostile aircraft appeared. Gradually, dominating all other sound, came the dull drone of bombers, flying low; but the guns went on firing, five rounds per gun per minute, for they were supporting an infantry attack. The first stick of bombs fell around the gun I was watching. Some of its crew were hit. The dry bush roared into flame, which spread instantly to the camouflage nets over the gun. It vanished from my sight in smoke and flame. Yet from the very midst of that inferno, at the exact intervals, came the flash and thud of the gun firing. Five rounds per gun per minute. Never a falter, never a second out. No weak link there; discipline held.

Any soldier who has courage, endurance, skill at arms, adaptability and discipline, will be a very efficient soldier but he will not be the British soldier, for he has something more.

It may seem strange to talk of gentleness as a soldierly quality, but it is — and he has it. Time and again the British soldier has combined real toughness in hardship and battle with gentleness to the weak, the defeated, the unhappy. Our bitterest enemies would rather be occupied by British troops than by any others. The British soldier is, bless him, a grim fighter but a bad hater.

He moves amid strange races and surroundings with an unarrogant assurance that radiates confidence. In famines, epidemics, earthquakes, floods, he has earned the dumb gratitude of millions. Thousands he has protected against their own violence and fanaticism — often with poor reward.

One sweltering afternoon, in the Red Fort at Delhi a company of British infantry was hurriedly falling in. There was a riot in the city, Hindu against Moslem. Heads were being broken, men stabbed, shops looted and burned. As the troops struggled into their equipment an officer said, "Now remember, in this quarrel you are neutral." A young soldier turned to his Sergeant, "Wot did 'e mean by nootral, Sergeant ?', he asked. "Nootral my lad," replied the N.C.O., "Nootral means that when you go down that adjectival bazaar, you're just as likely to be 'it by a Mo'amedan brick as by a 'Indue brick."

Unruffled by brickbats or bouquets, the soldier has marched across history, dominating the scene. Success that might turn another's head he greets with studied understatement; disaster that would appal most he meets with a jest, for his courage is always laced with humour. With his own brand of humour that is part of him and that he has kept, quick topical, and good-natured through the centuries.

There was a Grenadier at Fontenoy who, as the French presented their muskets for a devastating volley, intoned, "For what we are about to receive may the Lord make us truly thankful." He must have been brother to the freezing British fighting man, crouching under a Korean blizzard, who exclaimed, "I wish to Heaven the Iron Curtain was windproof!"

Many countries produce fine soldiers, whose achievements rival those of our own. It is character that the British soldier shows beyond others the marks of greatness. Courage, endurance, skill, adaptability, discipline they may have, but none blends these qualities together as he does with this leaven gentleness and humour. Nor has any other soldier his calm unshakeable confidence of victory.

The character of the British soldier is his own but in his achievements he has owed much to his officers. The regimental officers of the British Army have in all soldierly qualities, in self-sacrifice and in leadership been worthy of their men. They could not have, nor would they covet, higher praise.

Well, that's the British soldier, officer and man. We do take him for granted a bit, don't we? How many of you sitting there, listening to me, know more about the victories of your local football team than about those of your county regiment? Good luck to your football team, but give a hand to your Army too, for it is your Army, much more a part of the nation than it has ever been before in peace. And on it much more than a game may depend.

We have still forced on us now the grim necessity to look to our defences. That means for all of us in convenience and sacrifice, but before we grumble too much, let's remember two things. First, never was an untrained man of less value in war than he is today' and' second' if we deny ourselves to arm our forces, those arms will be going to the greatest of all fighting men — the British soldier.

The above is a broadcast by Field-Marshal Sir William Slim, delivered in 1951.It was published in the Wish Stream in the same year and in a foreword the Field-Marshal used the following words:

"This is a talk I gave recently on the wireless. If you read it, think how lucky you will be to lead such soldiers. Remember, too, that even the best soldiers are of little use without good officers — and our soldiers deserve the best. It's up to you to see that you are the best. You can be."

Field-Marshal Sir William Slim, Courage and other Broadcasts

The One Principle of War

War remains an art and, like all arts whatever its variation; will have its ending principles. Many men, skilled either with sword or pen and sometimes with both, have tried to expound these principles. I heard them once from a soldier of experience for whom I had a deep and well-founded respect. Many years ago, as a cadet hoping some day to be an officer, I was poring over "The Principles of War", listed in the old Field Services Regulations, when the Sergeant-Major came upon me. He surveyed me with kindly amusement. "Don't bother your head about all them things, me lad," he said. "There's only one principle of war and that's this. Hit the other fellow as quick as you can and as hard as you can, where it hurts him most, when he ain't looking.

Field-Marshal Sir William Slim, Defeat into Victory

The Infantryman

They marched back from the battle in the way of the infantry, their feet scarcely leaving the ground, their bodies rocking mechanically from side to side as if that was the only way they could lift their legs. You could see that it required the last ounce of their mental and physical energy to move their legs at all. Yet they looked as if they could keep on moving like that for ever.

Fred Majdalany, *The Monastery*

The British Soldier

Wars, therefore, will never cease, grievous though the thought may be. Yet, to descend again to lowly mundane things, its former outward manifestations seem likely to be transformed. It may well be that by new methods of scientific destruction the whole nature of armies may be changed. Infantry and Cavalry may vanish away and regiments and even armies in the old and honoured sense may cease to be. Then shall the British Army likewise perish and its place shall know it no more. It matters not. Were the Army to be swept tomorrow into nothingness, it has already done enough to give it rank with the legions of ancient Rome. And it will be remembered best not for its surpassing valour and endurance, not for its countless deeds of daring and its invincible stubbornness in battle, but for its lenience in conquest and its gentleness in domination. Let Wellington's phrase be repeated once more: "We are English and we pride ourselves on our deportment."

Empires decay and fall and the British Empire cannot escape the common lot. Already the Dominions are virtually independent. They will forget, as the Americans have already forgotten, what they owe to the British soldier; but not the less will his work for them remain. In India the rule of the British will fade in due time into a legend of stolid white men, very terrible in fight, who swept the land from end to end, enforcing for a brief space strange maxim of equity and government. The age may be hereafter mournfully recalled by the Indian peasant as that wherein his forefathers reaped what they had sown under the protection of the British soldier. When the Empire shall have passed away it is the British soldier's figure that will loom out eminent above all, the calm upholder of the King's peace.

And the historian of the dim future, summing up the whole story, may conclude it in such words as these. "The builders of this Empire despised and derided the stone which became the headstone of this corner. They were not worthy of such an Army. Two centuries of persecution could not wear out its patience; two centuries of thankless toil could not abate its ardour; two centuries of conquest could not awake it to insolence. Dutiful to its masters, merciful to its enemies, it clung steadfastly to its old simple ideals obedience, service, sacrifice.

Sir John Fortescue, A History of The British Army

Old Soldier's Secrets

He had the old soldier's knack of making himself comfortable anywhere. The rest of us used to crawl between our blankets in our shirts and trousers. Not Harry. He never slept in anything but crisp, white pyjamas. And he slept between sheets. And in spite of the general squalor, the sheets and the pyjamas always appeared to be spotless. In the early morning he always shaved long before anyone else, and appeared spruce and fresh as if straight from a shower; his trousers were invariably well creased, and his boots shiny. How he kept this up, no one ever knew. Old soldiers have their secrets which are not divulged to lesser mortals.

Fred Majdalany, The Monastery

The Irrepressible Soldier

I bade farewell to my right leg, and to my career as a soldier outside a trench at Gheluvelt, near Ypres, on 29th October, 1914. In the first Battle of Ypres, the British were outnumbered by seven to one. On the previous evening we took over trenches — not deep or elaborate ones — from the English regiment. I cannot say which regiment we relieved. Our Sergeant, on entering the trench, heard the last man as he was doing a hurried exit, say: "So long, Jock — not 'arf a nice place. Jack Johnson all bleeding day."

On that night there was no sleep as we had to dig and dig to improve the trench, and were being fired at all night. At 5 a.m. a group of us were standing in the open — everything had turned peaceful — admiring our now almost perfect French, when hell seemed let loose. All the guns in Flanders seemed to have suddenly concentrated on our particular sector of the British front. When the artillery fire subsided, Germans sprang from everywhere and attacked us. My Platoon held fast; we lost some good comrades. Then we were ordered to evacuate the trench, and assist to hold a trench on the flank where the fighting was fiercest. I was a sergeant, and was told to take and hold a certain part of the trench where the occupants had just been driven out. On rushing the trench, and leaping into it, I found that the dead were lying three deep in it. After taking bearings, I told the men to keep under cover and detailed one man, Ginger Bain, as "look-out". After what seemed ages, Ginger excitedly asked, 'How strong is the German Army?" I replied "Seven million. "Well," said Ginger, "here is the whole bloody lot of them making for us."

Sergeant Bell, quoted in Everyman at War

Arakan

The British Soldier must be driven to digging himself in the moment he occupies an area, and not to waste time in sightseeing, souvenir hunting and brewing tea.

Commander 36th Division 1944, quoted in Britain at Arms

Guns or Butter

When, in 1945, the Fourteenth Army was making its dash for Rangoon, we had not enough transport aircraft to keep the troops supplied with full rations and at the same time, give them all the ammunition they needed. So the rations went short. Then, just when we were strung out in the advance, a Japanese division appeared on the rear flank of one of our columns and put in a counter-attack.

For a bit the situation was tricky. At the time I was visiting a battery whose guns were firing all out to beat back a Japanese thrust. I stood watching one gunner, stripped to the waist, his lean, bronzed back glistening with sweat, as he slapped shells into the breach of a 25-pounder. There was a momentary pause in the firing, and I said to him: "I'm sorry you've got to do all this on half rations." He looked at me with a grin under his battered bush hat and answered: "Never you mind about that, sir ! Put us on quarter rations but give us the ammunition and we'll get you into Rangoon!"

Field-Marshal Sir William Slim, Courage and Other Broadcasts

Dressed to Kill

The better you dress a soldier, the more highly will he be thought of by the women, and consequently by himself.

Field-Marshal Lord Wolseley, The Soldier's Pocketbook, quoted in Britain at Arms

The Soldier Writes Home

WOOLWICH, February 26th, 1793

Dear Mother, Brother, Sister and aquentices,
This is the last from us in Ingland. I have just received orders for Germany under the command of the Duke of York, with 2,200 foot guards. We expect to embark tomorrow with 1 Captain, 4 Subalterns, 8 non-comishened Officers and 52 gunners to go with His Royal Highness as a Bodyguard of British Heroes. We are to lead the Dutch Prushen and Hanover Troops into the field, as there is none equal to the British Army. We are chosen troops sent by His Majesty to show an example to the other Troops, to go in front, & lead the combined army against the French which consists of 150,000 able fighten men. You may judge if we shall have anything to dow. I had the pleasure to conquer the French last war; but God knows how it will be this war. I cannot expect to escape the Bullets of my enemies much longer, as non has ever entered my flesh as yet. To be plain with you and not dishearten you, I don't expect to come off so cleare as I did last war. But it is death or honour. I expect to be a Gentleman or a Cripel. But you shall never see me to desteress you. If I cannot help you, I never shall destress you.
Dear Mother, take my family with me. Where I go, they must go. If I leave them, I should have no luck. My wife and 2 children

is in good health, & I in good spirits. Fear not for us. I hope God will be on our side.

Your Loven Son & Daughter,
GEO. & MARY ROBERTSON.

Sir John Fortescue, Following the Drum

N.C.O's Report

Ruthven Redoubt, 30th August, 1745.

HON GENERAL — This goes to acquaint you that yesterday there appeared in the little town of Ruthven about three hundred of the enemy, and sent proposals to me to surrender the redoubt upon Condition that I should have liberty to carry off bags and baggage. My answer was, "I am too old a soldier to surrender a garrison of such strength without bloody noses!" They threatened to hang me and my men for refusal. I told them I would take my chance. This morning they attacked me about twelve o'clock with about one hundred and fifty men; they attacked the fore-gate and sally-port. They drew off about half an hour after three. I expect another visit this night, but I shall give them the warmest reception my weak party can afford. I shall hold out as long as possible.

I conclude, Honourable General, with great respects,
Your most humble servant,
J. Molley, Sergt. 6th [Foot]

Quoted in Britain at Arms

Faith in the Regiment

Just "certain knowledge" . . . The men did not expect every officer to be a brilliant leader, and they strongly hoped he would not be a "pusher", but they expected him to put more than the next man into the general reservoir of courage. They did not look to him for ringing words of inspiration, but they liked to be reminded that they were the best mob in the line. No subaltern on the Western Front had read, or heard of, Wolseley's Pocket Book, but all grew to recognise the truth which Wolseley set out; "The soldier is a peculiar being that can alone be brought to the highest efficiency by inducing him to believe that he belongs to a regiment that is infinitely superior to the others round him." That was the Old Army's source of strength; and that faith in the regiment could be agreed through twenty battalions with very little dilution.

E. S. Turner, Gallant Gentlemen

MAN MANAGEMENT

Man Management – Today's problems

In this nuclear age the task of the officer in winning the respect and active co-operation of his men both in peace and war is even more vital than ever before. He MUST be the leader to whom men look for guidance and help when things go wrong, and who remains calm and unruffled under difficult, trying and sometimes dangerous circumstances. A leader to obtain such respect and co-operation must secure complete moral ascendancy over his men by the application of the following:

A deep understanding of each and all of the men under his command, their background and home life, their aspirations, their difficulties, their hopes and fears. An understanding of his platoon or equivalent unit en bloc is of little use as it is the man's personality that counts, and it is the officer's task to find this out.

A complete knowledge of his job, and this knowledge is chiefly gained through experience this means hard work and study, whether it be tactics, interior economy, administration or anything else that comes his way.

A high moral standard, including, above all, complete loyalty to those above him and absolute service to those under him.

If an officer is to be able to understand his men, it is essential that he gains their respect, otherwise they will never take him into their confidence. Many officers are shy in establishing the necessary bond of sympathy and are slow to show their men by their own behaviour that they are worthy of respect.

In short, the secret of good man management is proper understanding of every man under command, based on a secure foundation of his respect for your ability and integrity, and his confidence in your judgement.

Based on an extract from the R.M.A. Sandhurst study, Morale, Leadership Discipline

Know your Men

You will soon have bars on your shoulders; I've got things on mine that you've never seen before — but they both mean that we are officers. We have no business to set ourselves up as officers unless we know more about the job in hand that the men we are leading. If you command a small unit, like a platoon, you ought to be able to do anything you ask any man in it to do better than he can. Know the bolts and nuts of your job, but above all know your men. When you commend a platoon you ought to know each man in it better than his own mother does. You must know which man responds to encouragement, which is reasoning, and which needs a good kick in the pants. Know your men.

Field-Marshal Sir William Slim, Courage and other Broadcasts (extracts from an address to Cadets at West Point)

Peace of Mind

When a soldier is at war, his mind should be at peace.

Lord Moran

Health

I consider nothing in this country so valuable as the life and health of the British soldier.

Wellington in India, 1803.

Men

In India the men of the Army generally are looked upon as many pieces of one great machine that is passive in the hands of the engineer; and as to sense or feeling, that is not thought of. The private soldier is looked upon as the lowest class of animal, and only fit to be ruled with the cat o'nine tails and the provost-sergeant. Such a course is not likely wither to improve or to correct their morals, and I am sorry to say that it is very bad.

Private Robert Waterfield 32nd Foot, 1887

The Leader must know his Men

The matter of personal contact between commissioned officers and their men enters into leadership in so many ways that it is hardly possible to condense it into a single brief discussion.

When Alexander Pope wrote that "The proper study of mankind is man," he coined a fine motto for the art of personal leadership. For the crux of personal leadership is the leader's knowledge of his men — and knowledge of men has as its cornerstone an intelligent understanding of human nature.

An officer must therefore know his men, individually as well as collectively. To be able to lead their minds he must know what they really think — and he cannot possess this knowledge without first having entered to a certain extent into their lives, hopes, joy, fears and sorrows. If he does this with common sense it is no more subversive of discipline than the kindness of a father is destructive of his son's obedience.

A company officer should know every man in his organisation by name. To hail an individual as "You man" or "Hey, you !" is belittling. The enlisted man feels that he is just another man in the ranks with a serial number — an unimportant cog in which his superior has no personal interest. To use his name without his title in speaking to a non-commissioned officer, produces much the same effect. "Corporal Jones" or "Sergeant Kelly" is the right way. Every human being responds to the recognition of his personality, and his ability or achievement or experience as indicated by his rank.

Much can be learned about individual men by studying their service records and qualification cards. Visits to regimental headquarters to study Soldiers' Qualification Cards could well be made mandatory, for through them a company officer can get a comprehensive picture of the make-up of his unit. But these things are not enough by themselves. The man himself must be studied. The company officer should know his regional and temperamental characteristics, his weaknesses and strengths, his hopes and apprehensions. He should know something of the lives of his men before they enlisted, their families. Their educational and vocational backgrounds. He should constantly endeavour to know their states of mind, their attitudes towards their service and all the minor things which tend to raise or lower their morale.

The leader should weigh and consider every individual in his unit — his physical, mental and moral qualities; his appearance; his manner and performance of duty. This kind of sizing up is a task that is never completed. It is an unending job, both because first impressions may be enormous and because every enlisted man will inevitably become better or worse (and also because in peace or war there is a continual flow of recruits or replacements into every unit). If an officer thus reviews his first impressions in the tight of later daily contact and observation, he will improve and perfect his ability to analyse character.

Much of this necessary knowledge can only be attained from the men themselves. If an enlisted man is formally questioned he will often have only a minimum to say. He will do the same thing if he lacks confidence in his officer. The ability of an officer to talk to an enlisted man in a way that shows an understanding of him as a man is a sure approach to his confidence. And when it seems best, the official military relationship can be temporarily set aside — and a man put at ease and told to sit down to talk things over.

Personal information that an officer learns about other men of a unit from his non-commissioned officer leaders and other sources should be carefully weighed by him. Sometimes such information is heavily coloured. Too, it is destructive of morale for the men of a unit to feel that their leader may have snoopers or "white rats" in the unit, which is sometimes true in the unit of a leader who has the wrong ideas of leadership.

A few officers seem to possess an almost instinctive ability to find out the strengths and weaknesses of their men; but most of them must approach the task consciously and deliberately. For a company officer to ignore this constant study of human beings that make up his unit is for him to run the risk of disaster in battle itself, this through lack of a vital knowledge.

As a leader gains knowledge of his men he will always find out things about certain ones in the course of normal observation and without any prying on his part, that will in no way seem to him admirable — in fact, things that will often seem the opposite. These will, of course, be the ordinary weaknesses of humankind which any leader must freely acknowledge to exist, must look upon with reasonable tolerance, and must never permit himself to judge narrowly and harshly. If he does misjudge such traits he will find himself building up prejudices against individual subordinates who may well have the stuff within them that it takes to carry out their missions when it comes to combat itself.

Numerous examples of this have come to light among combat units in the present war. Many so-called "eight-balls" have gone out against Japs and Germans and covered themselves with glory, though, of course, many have not turned out well at all. How men behave against enemy fire is the criterion of final judgment; yet it cannot be recognised one way or the other by superficial acquaintance with a man. The leader must study all of his men with "the pay-off" in view.

Every leader must indeed constantly remember that his own ideals of conduct may not be those under which a particular member of his command has been brought up or accustomed to observe. This, of course, applies to many of the things already discussed — language, manner, and the like. For example, a big-talking, loud-mouthed, bragging soldier is not necessarily nine-tenths made up of wind. He may simply be good and know it, though he possesses the weakness of not being able to keep the news to himself. On the other hand, the mild-mannered, soft-spoken man who seems uncertain of himself and is never in the forefront, often creating in the leader's mind even an unpleasant appearance of ineffectuality, may simply be a man who shrinks from the limelight or who shrinks from added responsibilities because he thinks they will give him extra work.

Impatience with human foibles is to be found in greatest degree in young officer leaders whose ideals and desire for perfection are sometime higher than the present state of mankind will warrant. Such leaders especially must be careful to weigh their men in terms of battle results — and not in terms of the more or less rigid standards of conduct which they themselves have learned to follow and to think of as admirable.

Knowledge of the strengths and weaknesses of his men is one element of leadership that a leader can hardly possess too fully, for its results are always positive and never negative. The ability of an officer to predict, many reaction under various conditions must be based almost entirely upon the officer's first-hand knowledge of the man concerned. And from close observation of his unit he can often predict with accuracy how the entire organisation will react. He can thus not only forecast but even create reaction and conduct.

A study of psychology and psychiatry from standard books, such as "Psychology for the Fighting Man", and "Psychology for the Armed Services", is useful as in adjunct to the officer's practical experience with his men. Such studies will also give him a clearer knowledge of his own real or potential troubles, for the leader must have a knowledge of himself as well as of his men. Every officer in combat must know first aid; he must know, for example, how to apply a tourniquet. These practical life-saving measures are as much psychological as physical in their effect. He must also know the primary rules used by psychiatrists in the presence of combat neurosis. Of these two types of first aid, the second is even more important than the first. The good leader should know as much about practical psychiatry as strategy and tactics, since that science will provide him with a knowledge of the worst possibilities as well as the best possibilities of his men.

Colonel Munson, Leadership for American Army Leaders

Nothing to Worry About

In this surprising journey, nothing seemed to have been forgotten.

Parker says:
We frequently marched three sometimes four days successively and halted one day. We generally began our march about three in the morning, proceeded about four leagues or four-and-a-half by

day, and reached our ground about nine. As we marched through the countries of our allies, commissaries were appointed to furnish us with all manner of necessaries for man and horse; these were brought to the ground before we arrived, and the soldiers had nothing to do but to pitch their tents, boil their kettles and lie down to rest. Surely never was such a march carried on with more order and regularity and with less fatigue both to man and horse.

(This is a comment on Marlborough's march to the Danube.)
Sir Winston Churchill, Marlborough, His Life and Times

Victuals

It is very necessary to attend to detail, and to trace a biscuit from Lisbon into a man's mouth on the frontier, and to provide for its removal from place to place, by land and by water, or no military operations can be carried on.

Wellington, quoted in Britain at Arms

Food and its Significance

I don't think I shall ever grumble about food again. Certainly our men became thoroughly self-sufficient, even the worst of them, whether at cooking, at washing their clothes or anything else. I was immoderately pleased at the tribute of a Commodore of Convoys, who on three separate voyages had brought home Chindits finishing their time. He said that he hid never known men so cheerful, so willing, and so well able to look after themselves to their own satisfaction; and he contrasted them favourably with troops drawn from the same kind of homes and environment whom he had taken to South-East Asia each time on his outward voyage, and who, he said, were both helpless and discontented. I suggested that the reason might be partly due to the fact that the Chindits were homeward bound, and the others war-ward; but he insisted that the difference was more profound than that: it was the difference between men who had been used to having everything done for them and men who had learned the fundamentals.

I would say without hesitation that lack of food constitutes the biggest single assault upon morale. It is rarely noticed in the many books that have been written, and the many speeches delivered, upon that subject. Lord Moran, whose lectures on the subject of courage over many years lately culminated in a book, makes no mention of it. Apart from its purely chemical effects upon the body, it has woeful effects upon the mind. One is the dismal condition of having nothing to look forward to. Man is still an animal, and consciously or unconsciously he is always looking forward to his next meal. In this state, one finds one self saying: "I'm looking forward to something: what is it?" Then comes the cynical answer, "Eating; and there is nothing to eat, and there isn't going to be anything to eat." Then sets in a dreadful gloom; one wrenches the mind away from it, but in a few minutes the question asks itself again, and the same answer chills the spirit. At last the thought is there all the time, and only now and then is a new question asked, "Is there no hope of food?" To this there is one triumphant and tyrannical answer, "None".

The merest promise or hope of food will keep one going a long time. Christopher Buiney, writing of his time in Buchenwald in The Dungeon Democracy, says "A man who is really hungry, and who can calculate that tomorrow or the day after or even next week he will be given an extra 200 grammes of bread or an extra litre of soup, lives on that hope and stifles — the despair of hopelessness." I shall never forget the new lease of life granted to my servant Peter Dorans and me when, turning out my pack, we found fourteen grains of rice, spilt from some long forgotten ration, lying black and dirty at the bottom. We cooked them in a tablespoonful of water, and drew new strength and hope from sharing them.

When the hope of food is gone, a new assault develops upon the defences of the mind. This takes the form of a growing dread that soon your weakness may reach the pitch where it will overwhelm you. There is no more heart-rending sight than the man who finally falls, or the man whose struggles to resume his feet are fruitless. You can either remain with him and share his fate, or you must leave him where he lies, assert your leadership, rally your men and push on, one fewer. Your job is to get as many men to safety as you can. There can surely be no greater burden on the narrowing shoulders of leadership than this experience. I will write of it no more; but I think it proper that the race to which these men belonged should know what they suffered without complaining on its behalf. Of all the men whom I have had to leave wounded, sick or starving, not one reproached me, or made the dreadful duty harder than it already was.

Brigadier Bernard Fergusson, *The Wild Green Earth*

Games

Sixty years ago, if not longer, officers and men were playing in the same regimental team at cricket, but football was confined to schools and universities. Since then football has grown into a national pastime, in which the Army eagerly takes part; and the officers, not content with working with their men, have steadily played with them. In other armies such an association of all ranks on a common footing might be regarded as dangerous to discipline. In the British Army an officer who has led his men to victory

in a football match will be the more devotedly followed by them in
a sterner field.

Sir John Fortescue, A History of The British Army

Behaviour

It is, indeed, singular, how a man loses or gains caste with his comrades from his behaviour, and how closely he is observed in the
field.The officers, too, are commented upon and closely observed.
The men are very proud of those who are brave in the field, and
kind and considerate to the soldiers under them. An act of kindness done by an officer has often during the battle been the cause
of his life being saved.

Recollections of Rifleman Harris, Ed. H. Curling

NAAFI

Thus came into being what was known as the Expeditionary Force
Canteen, better known by its initials as the E.F.C. Its story cannot
here be even briefly set down, but it has the air of a romance rather
than of sober fact. The Expeditionary Force Canteen on the Western Front began with a single motor car and ended with a fleet of
four hundred and fifty. "It spread the table for the entire British
Expeditionary Force from the mess at General Headquarters to
the private soldiers' billets." And, not content with France, it followed the Army to Italy, to Gallipoli, to Salonica, to Palestine, to
Mesopotamia, even to the Arctic Circle. The range of its activities
was too wide and its volume of business too colossal to allow of
detailed mention here. Every commander in the field testified to

its efficiency and to its value in maintaining the cheerfulness and contentment of the troops. It bore its share in keeping mutiny at a distance. Yet it cost the country practically nothing, and returned huge revenues to officers and men.

Nor was even this the limit of its usefulness. Its success was so great that its principles were applied at home as well as abroad; and thus there grew up a gigantic organisation which reckoned its volume of trade by tens of millions sterling. The Navy and Air Force begged to be admitted to its privileges; and, when the war was ended, this organisation was permanently established as the Navy, Army and Air Force Institute. Wherever men of these three forces are to be found, there is a branch of the Institute to minister to their comfort, charging the lowest possible prices and returning the revenues to them. Be it specially noted that the Institute is not a department of the State. It is managed by the men who controlled the Expeditionary Force Canteen, that is to say, by the staff of the Canteen and Mess Co-operative Society. It has grown up in spite of the State, and is untainted by the hand of the politician. In its origin it was built up by a few humble regimental officers for the benefit of the soldier, and in its development it fulfils, and more than fulfils, their own declared purpose. The Institute belongs to the officers and men of the Navy, Army and Air Force, and to them alone. They are responsible for the management and for the disposal of its revenues. It is their very own. There is nothing like it to be found in any country in the world. It is the crowning work of the regimental officer for the Army.

Sir John Fortescue, A History of The British Army.

DUTY AND SERVICE

British Officers

From its earliest days the efficiency and the success of the standing army of Great Britain Lave been largely derived from the high qualifications of many of its officers. Practically every important campaign has produced at least one great leader, and many good ones; and almost all of them have been well educated. The training of some, such as Cromwell, Marlborough, and Clive, has been altogether practical; their wits sharpened and their intellect strengthened, as was also the case with Nelson and St. Vincent, by long and varied experience. These, however, are the exceptions, and it is not to be overlooked that their natural genius for war was of the highest order. The majority, including Wolfe and Wellington, have been deep students of the military art, relying not merely on the knowledge derived from their own personal practise and conclusions, but assimilating the practice and conclusions of the great captains. The era of Napoleon, when war first became a science, was peculiarly prolific, so far as the British army was concerned, in characters so trained. Wellington's lieutenants in the Peninsula and his colleagues in India were as earnest and as industrious as himself, and the tradition of hard work they handed down, though at times obscured, was never completely lost to sight. At no time was the importance of study more generally accepted as a guiding principle than at the end of the nineteenth century. The brilliant successes of Moltke and his Prussians, due almost entirely to a thorough knowledge of war and its practical application, had rekindled the torch. Competitive examination both for first commissions and the staff gave an impulse to intellectual activity; while the influence and example of Field-Marshal Lord Wolseley, the best-read soldier of his time, who from 1882 onwards was the moving spirit in the path of progress, had a marked effect upon the younger generation. Apathy became unfashionable, hard work the rule; study was no longer considered useless; and the professional acquirements of the officers reached a far higher standard than they had attained since Waterloo.

The standard, however, might easily have been higher still. Zeal was never lacking in the army. The troops had always been well disciplined and well drilled. The internal economy of the different units was everywhere admirable. The health and comfort of the men liere most carefully looked to; and the rivalry between regiments, and often between squadrons and companies, though confirmed to the exercises of the parade ground, to soldierly bearing, and to good conduct, was a token not only of a strong esprit de corps but of a strong sense of duty and professional pride among the regimental officers. They were supported, it is true, by an excellent body of non-commissioned officers; but although these men, who have been rightly styled the backbone of the army, furnished an invaluable link between the private soldier and the higher grades, their powers were strictly limited; they were merely assistants to their superiors; and it was impossible, under the system of regimental administration, that they could become their substitutes. Thus between the company officer and the rank and file no obstruction whatever existed, and in no army were their personal relations, especially on foreign service, closer, or more constant.

No incident is more familiar in our military history than the stubborn resistance of the British line at Waterloo. Through the long hours of the midsummer day, silent and immovable the squares and squadrons stood in the trampled corn, harassed by an almost incessant fire of cannon and of musketry, to which they were forbidden to make reply. Not a moment but heard some cry of agony; not a moment but some comrade fell headlong in the furrows. Yet as the bullets of the skirmishers hailed around them, and the great round shot tore through the tight-packed ranks, the word was passed quietly. "Close in on the centre, men"; and as the sun neared his setting, the regiments, still shoulder to shoulder, stood fast upon the ground they had held at noon. The spectacle is characteristic. In good fortune and in ill it is rare indeed that a British regiment does not hold together, and this indestructible cohesion, best of all the qualities that an armed body can possess, is based not merely on hereditary resolution, but on mutual confidence and mutual respect. The man in the ranks has implicit faith in his officer, the officer an almost unbounded belief in the valour and discipline of his men; . . .

Colonel Henderson, The Science of War

An Extract from General Orders

St. Perth November, 1813.

The commander of the Forces cannot sufficiently express his disapprobation of the conduct of Lieut. _____. The duties required from the junior ranks of the officers in the army, however easy of execution, are highly important to the welfare of the soldier, and are essential to the public interest, and they cannot be neglected without injury to both.

The Commander of the Forces trusts that what has happened to Lieut. will be a warning to others, to consider their professional duty their first object, and not to allow any idle pursuit to induce them to stay away from their regiment and neglect their duty.

Lieutenant-Colonel J. Gurwood, Wellington's Dispatches

The Warren Hastings

But I shall add just one story, a very short one, of the wreck of the Warren Hastings, which was carrying four companies of the King's Royal Rifle Corps and as many of the York and Lancaster Regiment, on the island of Reunion in 1987. When the ship struck, sentries of the Rifles were at once posted at various points on the lower deck, to guard the access to the spirit room and such like; and there they remained while boats were lowered to take the battalion ashore. The water rose steadily upon them inch by inch, and had reached their chests, when at last an officer came to summon them also, last of all, to take their place in the boats. He collected them all, as he thought, but in the noise and darkness he missed one man and left him behind. The man saw his comrades disappear up the ladder, and the officer about to follow them, and not till then did he ask, without quitting his post, "Beg pardon, sir, may I come too ?" If ever you hear any man speak lightly of military discipline, tell him that story, for that Rifleman is worthy to be placed alongside the Roman sentry at Pompeii.

Sir John Fortescue, Military History Lectures delivered at Trinity college, Cambridge

Action This Day

My rule was always to do the business of the day in the day.

Wellington to the Earl Stanhope, 1835

Manchester Hill

The late temporary Lieutenant-Colonel Wilfred Elstob, DSO, MC, 16th Battalion, Manchester Regiment.

For most conspicuous bravery, devotion to duty and self-sacrifice during operations at Manchester Redoubt, near St. Quentin, on the 21st March, 1918.

During the preliminary bombardment he encouraged his men in the posts in the Redoubt by frequent visits, and when repeated attacks developed controlled the defence at the points threatened, giving personal support with revolver, rifle and bombs. Single-handed he repulsed one bombing assault, driving back the enemy and inflicting severe casualties.

Later, when ammunition was required, he made several journeys under severe fire in order to replenish the supply. Throughout the day Lieutenant-Colonel Elstob, although twice wounded, showed the most fearless disregard of his own safety, and by his encouragement and noble example inspired his command to the fullest degree.

The Manchester Redoubt was surrounded in the first wave of the enemy attack, but by means of the buried cable Lieutenant-Colonel Elstob was able to assure his Brigade Commander that "The Manchester Regiment will defend Manchester Hill to the last".

Some time after, this post was overcome by vastly superior forces,and this very gallant officer was killed in the final assault, having maintained to the end the duty which he had impressed on his men — namely, "Here we fight and here we die".

He set throughout the highest example of valour, determination, endurance, and fine soldierly bearing.

London Gazette, 9th June, 1919

The Commander

Sir Ian Hamilton in describing Lord Roberts' powers ol personal leadership and writing of his "affection — a very deep affection — for mankind, and especially for those for whom he was or had been responsible", gives an example:

"Thus, after an exhausting march, Lord Roberts reaches camp with a sharp go of lever on him. Do you suppose he would go to his tent and lie down? Not much! There he would sit, half-dead, his staff simply writhing in their saddles with fatigue whilst he watched the long column march in for four long hours aid exchanged kindly greeting with any particularly exhausted."

General Sir Ian Hamilton, The Commander

The Adjutant

He was open-hearted, manly, friendly, and independent, a most gallant and zealous officer, and much devoted to his own corps. He neither cringed to, nor worshipped any man, but did his duty manfully, and with impartiality — two qualities inestimable in an adjutant.

Lieutenant-Colonel J. Leech

The Prisoner of War

The George Cross. Lieutenant Terence Edward Waters (463718) (deceased), The west Yorkshire Regiment (The prince of Wales Own), attached The Gloucestershire Regiment.

Lieutenant waters was captured subsequent to the Battle of the Imjin River, 22nd-25th April, 1951. By this time he had sustained a serious wound in the top of the head and yet another most painful wound in the arm as a result of this action.

On the journey to Pyongyang with other captives, he set a magnificent example of courage and fortitude in remaining with wounded other ranks on the march, whom he felt it his duty to care for to the best of his ability.

Subsequently, after a journey of immense hardship and privation, the party arrived at an area west of Pyongyang adjacent to P.W. Camp 12 and known generally as "The Caves" in which they were held captive. They found themselves imprisoned in a tunnel driven into the side of a hill through which a stream of water flowed continuously, flooding a great deal of the floor, in which were packed a great number of South Korean and European prisoners-of-war in rags, filthy crawling with lice. In this cavern a number died daily from wounds, sickness, or merely malnutrition: They fed on two small meals of boiled maize daily. Of medical attention there was none.

Lieutenant Waters appreciated that few, if any, of his numbers would survive these conditions, in view of their weakness and the absolute lack of attention for their wounds. After a visit from a North Korean Political Officer, who attempted to persuade them to volunteer to join a prisoner-of-war group known as "Peace Fighters" (that is, active participants in the propaganda movement against their own side) with a promise of better food, of medical treatment and other amenities as a reward for such activity — an offer that was refused unanimously — he decided to order his men to pretend to accede to the offer in an effort to save their lives. This he did, giving the necessary instructions to the senior other rank with the British party, Sergeant Hoper, that the men would go upon his order without fail.

Whilst realising that this act would save the lives of his party, he refused to go himself aware that the task of maintaining British prestige was vested in him.

Realising that they had failed to subvert an officer with the British party, the North Koreans now made a series of concerted efforts to persuade Lieutenant Waters to save himself by joining the camp. This he steadfastly refused to do. He died a short time after.

He was a young, inexperienced officer, comparatively recently commissioned from The Royal Military Academy, Sandhurst, yet he set an example of the highest gallantry.

London Gazette, 9th April, 1954

Officers

It is singular how a man loses or gains caste with his comrades from his behaviour, and how closely he is observed in the field. The officers, too are commented upon and closely observed. The men are very proud of those who are brave in the field, and kind and considerate to the soldiers under them. An act of kindness done by an officer has often during the battle been the cause of his life being saved . . . I know from experience that in our army the men like best to be officered by gentlemen, men whose education has rendered them more kind in manners than your course officer, sprung from obscure origin, and whose style is brutal and overbearing.

Recollections of Rifleman Harris, Peninsula, 1808

"*Greater Love*"

Nearby, I met Bob (the RMO) returning to the Regimental Aid Post from a talk with the Colonel. The signallers had already destroyed their sets, and Harry was stamping on the ashes of the codebook he had just burnt. We were all ready to move. In small groups, the Headquarters split up and ran over the ridge. When they had gone, I, too, came up on, to the ridge crest and prepared to descend the other side. Bob was standing alone by the path that led to the steep slopes below us.

"Come on, Bob," I said. "We're about the last to go. You ought to have gone before this. The Colonel will be off in a minute and that will be the lot." He looked at me for a moment before saying:

"I can't go. I must stay with the wounded."

For a few seconds I did not comprehend his meaning: we were all making our way out — there seemed a very fair chance that some of us would make it: to stay here was to stay certainly for capture, possibly for death, when the Chinese launched their final assault on the position. And then I realised that he had weighed all this — weighed it all and made a deliberate choice: he would place his own life in the utmost jeopardy in order to remain with the wounded at the time when they would need him most. Somewhere, the words appear, "Greater love hath no man than this . . ." I knew now exactly what those words meant. Too moved to speak again, I clapped my hand upon his shoulder and went on.

Captain Farrar-Hockley, *The Edge of The Sword*

COURAGE

Courage

Courage is rightly esteemed the first of human qualities . . . because it is the quality which guarantees all others.

Sir Winston Churchill

Facets of Courage

Courage is a moral quality; it is not a chance gift of nature like an aptitude for games. It is a cold choice between two alternatives, the fixed resolve not to quit; an act of renunciation which must be made not once but many times by the power of the will. Courage is will-power.

Likewise in the trenches a man's will-power was his capital and he was always spending, so that wise and thrifty company officers watched the expenditure of every penny lest their men went bankrupt.

I contend that fortitude in war has its roots in morality; that selection is a search for character, and that war itself is but one more test — the supreme and final test if you will — of character. Character as Aristotle taught is a habit, the daily choice of right instead of wrong; it is a moral quality which grows to maturity in peace and is not suddenly developed on the outbreak of war . . . Man's fate in battle is worked out before the war begins.

Lord Moran, *The Anatomy of Courage*

What is Courage?

I don't believe there's any man who, in his heart of hearts, wouldn't rather be called brave than have any other virtue attributed to him. And this elemental, if you like unreasoning, male attitude is a sound one, because courage is not merely a virtue; it is the virtue. Without it there are no other virtues. Faith, hope, charity, all the rest don't become virtues until it takes courage to exercise them. Courage is not only the basis of all virtue; it is its expression. True, you may be bad and brave, but you can't be good without being brave.

Courage is a mental state, an affair of the spirit, and so it gets its strength from spiritual and intellectual sources. The way in which these spiritual and intellectual elements are blended, I think, produces roughly two types of courage. The first, an emotional state which urges a man to risk injury or death — physical courage. The second, a more reasoning attitude which enables him coolly to stake career, happiness, his whole future on his judgment of what he thinks either right or worth while — moral courage.

Now, these two types of courage, physical and moral, are very distinct. I have known many men who had marked physical courage, but lacked moral courage. Some of them were in high positions, but they failed to be great in themselves because they lacked it. On the other hand, I have seen men who undoubtedly possessed moral courage very cautious about physical risks. But I have never met a man with moral courage who would not, when it was really necessary, face bodily danger. Moral courage is higher and a rarer virtue than physical courage.

To be really great, a man — or a nation — must possess both forms of courage. In this the Japanese were an interesting study. No army has ever possessed massed physical courage as the Japanese did; its whole strength lay in the emotional bravery of the individual soldier. The Japanese generals shared their men's physical bravery to the full, but they lacked, almost to a man, moral courage. They had not the moral courage to admit when their plans had failed and ought to have been changed; to tell their superiors that their orders could not be carried out and retreat while there was still time. We played on this weakness and by it the Japanese commanders lost their battles and destroyed their armies.

All men have some degree of physical courage — it is surprising how much. Courage, you know, is like having money in the bank. We start with a certain capital of courage, some large, some small,

and we proceed to draw on our balance, for don't forget courage is an expendible quality. We can use it up. If there are heavy, and, what is more serious, if there are continuous calls on our courage, we begin to overdraw. If we go on overdrawing we go bankrupt — we break down. You can see this overdraft mounting clearly in the men who endure the most prolonged strains in war; the submarine complement, the infantry platoon, the bomber crew. First there comes a growing impatience and irritability; then a hint of recklessness, a sort of "Oh to hell with it chaps, we'll attack!" spirit; next, real foolhardiness, what the soldier calls, "asking for it"; and last, sudden changes of mood from false hilarity to black moroseness. If before that stage is reached the man's commander has spotted what is happening and pulled him out for a rest, he will recover and in a few months be back again as brave and as balanced as ever. The capital in his bank of courage will have built up and he can start spending again.

There are, of course, some people whose capital is so small that it is not worth while employing them in peace or war in any job requiring courage — they overdraw too quickly. With us these types are surprisingly few. Complete cowards are almost non-existent. Another matter for astonishment is the large number of men and women in any group who will behave in emergency with extreme gallantry. Who they will be you cannot tell until they're tested. I long ago gave up trying to spot potential V.C.'s by their looks, but, from experience, I should say that those who perform individual acts of the highest physical courage are usually drawn from one or two categories. Either those with quick intelligence and vivid imagination, or those without imagination and with minds fixed on the practical business of living. You might almost say, I suppose, those who live on their nerves and those who haven't got any nerves. The one suddenly sees the crisis, his imagination flashes the opportunity and he acts. The other meets the situation without finding it so very unusual and deals with it in a matter-of-fact way.

Long ago, in the First World War, when I was a bit more irresponsible, I served under an officer of vivid imagination. He was always fussing about dangers that usually didn't exist. Once after a day and half a night of his constant alarms I was so fed up that I disconnected the telephone in the advanced post I was holding. I wanted some sleep. I didn't get it. Within half an hour his imagination had painted the most frightful pictures of my position overrun by the enemy. He arrived with the reserve company to retake it. As he was my commanding officer I had some rather difficult explaining to do ! I thought he was just windy. A few days later he won the V.C. by a superb example of leadership and courage.

In this last war in Burma a young Gurkha won the V.C. At a critical moment when Japanese medium tanks had broken through our forward positions, he took his Piat — an anti-tank grenade discharger — and leaving cover moved forward over the open towards the tanks. He was shot in the hand, the shoulder and again badly in the leg, but he got to within thirty yards of the tanks and bumped off two of them' Later, when I saw him in hospital, I asked him why he had walked forward in the pen like that. He replied: "I'd been trained not to fire the Piat until I was certain of hitting. I knew I could hit at thirty yards, so I went to thirty yards !" He had had only one thought in his head — to get to thirty yards. Quite simple if you are not bothered by imagination.

Can courage be taught? I am sure in one sense physical courage can. What in effect you must do is train the man not to draw too heavily on his stock of courage. Teach him what to expect, not to be frightened by bogeys — by the unknown. If you send an untrained British soldier on patrol in the jungle, every time a branch creaks, every time there is a rustle in the undergrowth when an animal slinks across the track, when a bush moves in the wind, he will draw heavily and unnecessarily on his stock of courage. And he will come back a shaken man, with a report of no value. But if you train that man beforehand, let him live in the jungle, teach him its craft, then send him on patrol, he will come back with his balance of courage unimpaired and probably a couple of enemy helmets into the bargain.

To teach moral courage is another matter — and it has to be taught because so few, if any, have it naturally. The young can learn it from their parents, in their homes, from school and university, from religion, from other early influences, but to inculcate it in a grown-up who lacks it requires not so much teaching as some striking emotional experience — something that suddenly bursts upon him; something in the nature of a vision. That happens rarely, and that is why you will find that most men with morale courage learnt it by precept and example in their youth.

Now, I suppose because I am a soldier, I have talked most of courage in men at war, but the fighting man is the last to claim a monopoly in courage. Many a soldier this last war has steeled himself in battle with the thought of what his civilian fellow-countrymen and women were enduring and how they were enduring it. Whether women are braver than men I don't know, but I have always found them, when really tested, at least equally brave.

In the retreat from Burma in 1942, I was deeply proud of the troops who staggered into India, exhausted, ragged, reduced to a remnant, but carrying their weapons and ready to turn again and face the enemy. Yet the outstanding impression of courage I carried away from that desperate campaign was from the Indian women refugees. Day after day, mile after mile, they plodded on, through dust or mud, their babies in their arms, children clinging to their skirts, harried by ruthless enemies, strafed from the air, shelterless, caught between the lines in every battle, yet patient, uncomplaining, devoted, thinking only of their families — so very brave.

Now, without talking any nonsense about master races, as the Japanese and Germans did, it is a fact that races do vary in courage. Some are braver than others — and you jolly soon find out which they are when you fight them. At a guess I should say it depends mostly on where they have lived for the past five or six hundred years. If it has been in a land where it did not take much effort to get enough food, clothing and shelter for an easy life, they will not be conspicuously brave. If they have lived where life is so hard that it is a terrible struggle against Nature to keep any standard of living at all, then they will be brave in a few things — dangers to which they are inured — but not at all brave in others. It is the lands where Nature is neither too easy nor too cruel, where a man must work hard to live but where his efforts and his enterprise can bring him great rewards, that breed courage and where it becomes a natural tradition. And don't run away with the idea that this limits courage to Northern Europe and North America. Believe me — and I've fought both with and against them — some of the bravest races in the world aren't white at all.

And while nations vary in the amount of their courage, they vary too in its type. We, the British, have our own special kind of courage, the courage that goes on — and endurance is the very essence — of courage. Courage is a long-term virtue. Anyone can be brave for a little while. The British are no braver than the Germans, the French, the Italians or anybody else, but they are brave for a bit longer. This going-on being brave when most others would have given up has been the racial characteristic of our courage.

It is interesting to speculate how we have developed this particularly practical and effective kind of courage. I am inclined to think that, like so much in the world, it has been a matter of geography and history. We draw our racial stock almost wholly from Northern Europe, one of the good areas for natural courage, and our intellectual and cultural heritage almost entirely from the Mediterranean, the great source of enlightened thought and imagination. At any rate, in the great moments of our history, we have based our natural courage on faith, a belief that we worked or fought for the things that mattered — a decent life, the freedom of spirit. That has been our strength. And it remains our strength for the same courage which has seen us through the crisis of war is needed now to see us through the hardly less formidable difficulties of peace. How fortunate are we, then, that we come of a race that, whatever its faults, has never failed for want of courage!

Field-Marshal Sir William Slim, Courage and other Broadcasts

Character and Courage

A man of character in peace is a man of courage in war.

Lord Moran, The Anatomy of Courage

Fear

The first duty of a man is still that of subduing fear.

Thomas Carlyle, Lecture 1840, Heroes and Hero Worship

"Volunteering"

It is by no means sure that because a fellow volunteers for a dangerous job he will be good at it; it is not even sure that his heart will be in it. The motive that impels him may be one of a dozen. One can have nothing but sympathy for a lad, young keen and fit, who feels that he is missing the war, and volunteers for anything that comes his way. Brought up on tales of gallant deeds, he wants to assure himself that he too can stand discomfort and fear, and be capable of endurance through hardship and privation. But nobody can tell, until he has had experience of these things, what they will really be like; he may be sure that they are quite unlike whatever he has pictured. I interviewed many officers who volunteered for Chindit duty between the two Expeditions. A high proportion were young and keen, but wholly without experience. Of those I took, some turned out well; a few, whose imagination had built them a false picture of what endurance means, failed badly. The most useful type is that which has had some experience, didn't like it much, but wants to go again with eyes open, knowing something of what war is like, yet confident that he can stand another helping. The man who really enjoys hardship is a rarity and a freak.

Brigadier Bernard Fergusson, *The Wild Green Earth*

Immortal

"Dogs, would you live forever?"

Frederick The Great (to soldiers reluctant to advance)